Beauty

Wildflowers of the Canadian Prairies

Neil L. Jennings

Victoria Vancouver Calgary

Rocky Mountain Books   Rocky Mountain Books
#108 – 17665 66A Avenue   PO Box 468
Surrey, BC V3S 2A7   Custer, WA
www.rmbooks.com   98240-0468

Library and Archives Canada Cataloguing in Publication

Jennings, Neil L.
Prairie beauty : wildflowers of the Canadian Prairies / Neil L. Jennings.

Includes index.
ISBN 978-1-894765-84-8

1. Wild flowers—Prairie Provinces—Identification. I. Title.
QK203.P68J46 2007   582.1309712   C2007-900008-8

Library of Congress Control Number:
2006940305

Edited by Corina Skavberg
Proofread by Joe Wilderson
Book design by John Luckhurst GDL
Cover design by John Luckhurst GDL
Front cover photo by Neil L. Jennings
All interior photos by Neil L. Jennings except as otherwise noted

Printed in Hong Kong

Rocky Mountain Books acknowledges the financial support for its
publishing program from the Government of Canada through the Book
Publishing Industry Development Program (BPIDP), and the province
of British Columbia through the British Columbia Arts Council and the
Book Publishing Tax Credit.

ACKNOWLEDGEMENTS

When I began work on this book, I was aware that I would need
assistance in order to obtain the images necessary to complete the
project. In that regard I contacted a number of field naturalist
societies in various places in Western Canada and requested help
from their members. The responses to my inquiries were very
gratifying, and led me to a number of photographers who graciously
and generously contributed some of their work to the project.
Without that help, the book could not have been completed.
I understand that making a list of people to thank is a dangerous
procedure, the very real peril being that some deserving of thanks
will be omitted from the list, but here I go anyway, with apologies
to anybody I might miss. Particular thanks go to Glen Lee and Colin
Ladyka of Regina, Saskatchewan; Anne Elliott and Cliff Wallis of
Calgary, Alberta; Margot Hervieux and Elaine Nepstad of Grande
Prairie, Alberta; Russ Webb and Dallas Hoffman of Okotoks, Alberta;
Delta Fay Cruickshank, Joyce Johnson, and Roy and Minnie Johnson
of Yahk, British Columbia; the Fort McMurray Field Naturalists
Society; the Native Plant Society of Saskatchewan; the Edmonton
Natural History Club; the Peace Parkland Naturalists Society; the
Cross Conservation Area; and the Calgary Field Naturalist' Society.
I also must thank my wife, Linda, for her assistance, support,
patience, and companionship in the pursuit of the subjects of
this book.

This book is dedicated to our dear friend
Carol Baker, whose cheerfulness, class, and
pluck in the face of seemingly insurmountable
adversity stand as an inspiration to all of us.

CONTENTS

INTRODUCTION

This book is intended to be a guide for the non-botanist to the identification of wild flowering plants commonly found in the prairie environment of Western Canada. It is written for the edification and enjoyment of anybody who ventures outdoors and wishes to be able to identify the wild flowering plants they encounter there. The book contains a minimum of scientific jargon, and is directed at the user who has no particular back-ground in matters botanical. Encounters with wildflowers are, happily, inevitable and unavoidable when you are outside, and it is my sincere belief that most people wish to know something about the flowers they see. "Do you know what this flower is called?" is one of the most often asked questions when I meet people in the field. Hopefully, the user will be able to answer the question by reference to the contents of this book. Identification of unknown species is based on comparison of the unknown plant with the photographs contained in the book, augmented by the narrative descriptions associated with the species pictured. In many cases the exact species will be apparent, while in other cases the reader will be led to plants that are similar to the unknown plant, thus providing a starting point for further investigation. As a general rule, plant recognition is not hugely difficult, and I believe that most people will have a richer experience outdoors if they learn to recognize the wildflowers they encounter.

This book does not cover all of the species of wildflowers that exist on the prairies. I am not aware of any book that does that. Indeed, if all species were included, this book would be complicated to the extent that it may become cumbersome and ineffectual, and it also might be difficult to carry. There are, quite literally, thousands of species existent on the prairies. This book addresses the most common of those species—those that any hiker might encounter on any given day in season. Some books eschew imported (non-native) species, often opining that they are somehow less deserving of attention, less interesting, and/or less important than native species. I do not really understand this prejudice, and I certainly have not adopted it in compiling the book. There is a large number of "alien" species out there, some introduced accidentally, some intentionally, and some mysteriously, but the fact is, they *are* out there, and their identification is equally interesting to many outdoor enthusiasts. Some of the alien species are noxious weeds—that is, they are highly competitive in the environment, and can push out native species, most probably because they come from "away" and have no natural enemies in their new environment to keep them in check. Some of these species are invaders, in the truest sense of the word, and need to be held in check where possible, or, in some cases, even eradicated from their new home. In order to do that, however, correct identification is the paramount consideration before a counter-attack can commence. So, I have included them, perhaps not affectionately, but because they are there.

I own a number of wildflower guidebooks and have consulted them extensively over the years, even to the point of having some of them unravel at the binding and fall to pieces. As much as I have used such books, it has always occurred to me that they all share a couple of deficiencies for the non-botanist. First, the photographs in the books are usually too small and/or they lack the detail necessary to make identification easy, or even possible, in some cases. Second, the books are written by botanists and assume a level of botanical expertise in the reader that does not exist. In my view, what most people really want to know about wildflowers is "what is this thing?" and "tell me something interesting about it." Botanical detail, while interesting and enlightening to some of us, will turn off many people.

So I have set out to produce the best photographic representations I could obtain, together with some information about the plant that the reader might find interesting and that might assist the reader in remembering the names of the plants. This is not a book for scientists. It is a book for the curious. What I am attempting to do is assist people who want to be able to recognize and identify common wildflowers that they see while outdoors. I have tried to keep it simple, while making it interesting and enjoyable.

The plants depicted in the book are arranged first by colour, and then by family. This is a logical arrangement for the non-botanist because the first thing a person notes about a flower is its colour. All of the plants shown in the book are identified by their prevailing common names. Where I knew of other common names applied to any plant, I noted them. I have also included the scientific names of the plants. This inclusion is made to promote specificity. Common names vary significantly from one region to another; scientific names do not. If you want to learn the scientific names of the plants to promote precision, fine. If you do not want to deal with that, fine. Just be mindful that many plants have different common names applied to them depending on geography and local usage.

The prairie environment is geographically large and diverse. Some homogeneity exists, but there are also lots of anomalies too, such as the Cypress Hills in southern Alberta and Saskatchewan. There is also some overlap, with some plants appearing in the prairie community also appearing in floral communities of other vegetation zones. Happily, what you learn in the prairies might be readily transferable to other zones.

A few cautionary comments and suggestions:
Go carefully among the plants so as not to damage or disturb them.
In parks, stay on the established trails. In large measure, those trails exist to allow us to view the natural environment without trampling it to death.

Do not pick the flowers. Leave them for others to enjoy. Bear in mind that in national and provincial parks it is illegal to pick any flowers.

Do not attempt to transplant wild plants. Such attempts are most often doomed to failure.

Do not eat any plants or plant parts. To do so presents a potentially significant health hazard. Many of the plants are poisonous—some violently so.

Do not attempt to use any plants or plant parts for medicinal purposes. To do so presents a potentially significant health hazard. Many of the plants are poisonous—some violently so.

One final cautionary note—the pursuit of wildflowers can be addictive, though not hazardous to your health.

Neil L. Jennings
Calgary, Alberta

PLANT SHAPES AND FORMS

Parts of a Leaf

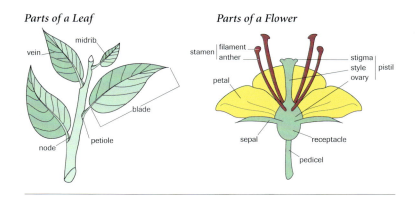

Parts of a Leaf

vein • midrib • blade • petiole • node

Parts of a Flower

Parts of a Flower

stamen { filament, anther } • petal • sepal • receptacle • pedicel • stigma, style, ovary } pistil

Leaf Arrangements

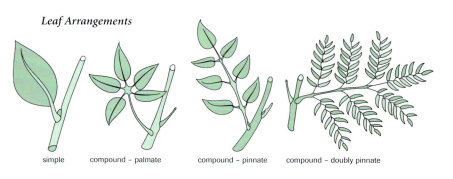

simple   compound – palmate   compound – pinnate   compound – doubly pinnate

Stem Arrangements

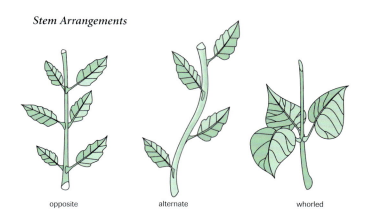

opposite   alternate   whorled

Leaf Shapes

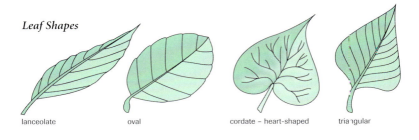

lanceolate   oval   cordate – heart-shaped   triangular

Leaf Margins

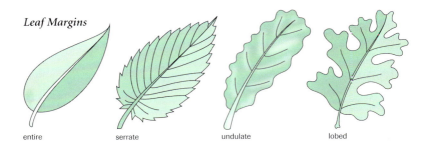

entire   serrate   undulate   lobed

Venation

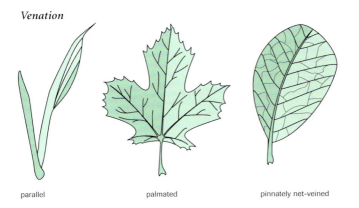

parallel   palmated   pinnately net-veined

TERRITORIAL RANGE OF WILDFLOWERS

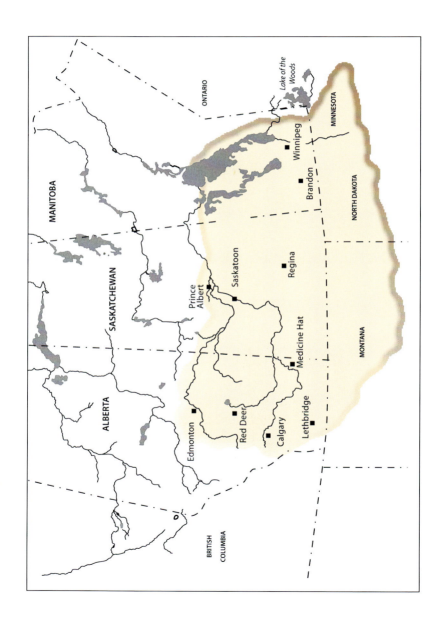

Yellow Flowers

This section includes flowers that are predominantly yellow when encountered in the field. The colour varies from bright yellow to pale cream. Some of the flowers in this section have other colour variations, and you might have to check other sections of the book to find the flower. For example, the Paintbrushes (*Castilleja* spp.) have a yellow variation, but they are most often encountered in a red colour and they have been pictured in that section for purposes of sorting.

Common Bladderwort
Utricularia vulgaris

BLADDERWORT FAMILY

This aquatic carnivorous plant is found in shallow water in sloughs, lakes, ditches, and ponds. It floats beneath the surface of the water, with a tangle of course stems and leaves. The long, branching, submerged stems have finely divided leaves that spread out like small nets. Attached to the leaves hang numerous small bladders that are actually traps for aquatic insects. When an insect swims into the bladders, small hairs are tripped which shuts the bladder, trapping the insect inside. The insects are then digested, providing a source of nitrogen for the plant. The yellow flowers appear on leafless stalks that extend above the surface of the water. The corolla of the flower is two-lipped, with brown stripes on the throat. The floral tube extends into a short, spur-like sac at the base.

The genus name, *Utricularia*, is derived from the Latin *utriculus*, which means "small bottle" or "little bag," a reference to the bladders on the plants. The species name, *vulgaris*, means "common."

Puccoon (Lemonweed)
Lithospermum ruderale

BORAGE FAMILY

A coarse perennial up to 50 cm high, this plant is firmly anchored to dry slopes and grasslands by a large woody taproot. The numerous leaves are sharp-pointed, lance-shaped, and clasp the stem. The small yellow flowers are partly hidden in the axils of the leaves near the top of the plant, and have a strong, pleasant scent. The stems and leaves are covered in long white hairs. The fruit is an oval, cream-coloured nutlet that is somewhat pitted, and resembles pointed teeth.

The genus name, *Lithospermum*, is derived from the Greek *lithos*, meaning "stone," and *sperma*, meaning "seed," a reference to the fruit of the plant. Indeed, another common name for the plant is Stoneseed. For centuries, some Native peoples used an extract of the plant for birth control. Natural estrogens in the plant suppress the release of certain hormones required for ovulation. The roots of the plant were used as a source of red dye. Another common name for the plant is Woolly Gromwell. A similar plant, Narrow-Leaved Puccoon (*L. incisum*) appears in similar habitat. It differs from this species in that the flowers of Narrow-Leaved Puccoon have petals which are fringed or toothed, not smooth like this species.

Western False Gromwell
Onosmodium molle

BORAGE FAMILY

A leafy perennial that grows up to 80 cm tall, this plant is found on gravel banks and dry slopes, and in dry woods in the southern part of the area. The leaves are numerous, sessile (stalkless), lance-shaped, prominently veined, and very hairy. The flowers are yellowish-white in colour and occur in crowded clusters in the top one-third of the stem. The long styles protrude from the flowers. The fruits are hard, pearly-white nutlets.

The genus name, *Onosmodium*, is derived from the plant's resemblance to some plants in the foul-smelling *Onosma* genus. *Onosma* means "smelling like an ass." The species name, *molle*, is derived from Latin and means "soft," a reference to the soft white hairs on the plant. Indeed, another common name applied to the plant is Softhair Marbleseed. The common name Western False Gromwell arises because this plant is thought to resemble plants in the *Lithospermum* genus (Puccoons), shown on page 3. Puccoons are often referred to as Gromwells.

Clustered Broom-Rape
Orobanche fasciculata

BROOM-RAPE FAMILY

This plant is a relatively rare parasitic perennial that grows to heights of 15 cm in grasslands and dry open forests, often using sagebrushes (*Artemisia* spp.) as host plants. The "leaves" on the plant are brownish scales. The flower stalks are fleshy, glandular-hairy, brown, and often yellowish or purple tinged. Three to ten flowers appear atop the stalks. The flowers have a purplish or yellowish tube-shaped corolla, with 2 lips, the upper being two-lobed, and the lower three-lobed.

The common name, Broom-Rape, comes from a related English species that is parasitic on scotch broom (*Cytisus scoparius*). The genus name, *Orobanche*, is derived from the Greek *orobos*, which means "clinging plant," and *ancho*, which means "to strangle," a reference to the plant's parasitic growth habit. The species name, *fasciculata*, is derived from the Latin *fascis*, which means "clustered" or "bundled," a reference to the bunched nature of the flowers. These plants get their nutrients from the host plant, therefore have no need for photosynthesis. It is no doubt overstating the case to imply that these plants are strangling or doing other violence to their host plants.

Yellow Buckwheat (Umbrella Plant)
Eriogonum flavum
BUCKWHEAT FAMILY

This fuzzy haired tufted perennial favours dry, often sandy or rocky outcrops, eroded slopes, and badlands. The leaves are dark green on top, but appear white to felty on the underside due to the dense hairs. The yellow flowers occur in compound umbels—umbrella shaped clusters—atop the stem. The common name for the plant, Umbrella Plant, is testimony to the shape of the inflorescence.

The genus name, *Eriogonum*, is derived from the Greek *erion*, meaning "wool," and *gony*, meaning "knee or joint." *Flavum* means "yellow." The plant has an unpleasant smell, but the nectar is relished by bees, and produces a strongly flavoured buckwheat-like honey.

Creeping Buttercup (Seaside Buttercup)
Ranunculus cymbalaria

BUTTERCUP FAMILY

This Buttercup spreads over the ground by slender, creeping stems or runners, similar to those of the Wild Strawberry. The leaf blades are long-stalked, egg- or heart-shaped, and have scalloped margins. The plant is found in moist meadows, on stream banks, and at the margins of lakes and ponds.

Buttercups are among the oldest of flower families, existing for millions of years before earliest man developed, and are considered one of the most primitive plant families. The cell structure of the petals is such that there is air in the cell vacuoles, and this is responsible for the "whiteness" seen on the petals. The genus name, *Ranunculus*, is from the Greek *rana*, which means "frog," a likely reference to the wetland or marshy habitat of many species of the family. The species name, *cymbalaria*, means "pertaining to cymbals," and is most probably a reference to the shape of the leaves.

Marsh-Marigold
Caltha palustris
BUTTERCUP FAMILY

Favouring wet meadows, woods, and bogs, the Marsh-Marigold is often found in shallow water of slow moving streams and ditches. The flower has 5–9 bright yellow, showy sepals, but no petals. The leaves are mostly basal and quite distinctive, being dark green, large, and round to kidney- or heart-shaped.

The common name is said to have come from "Mary's Gold," a reference to a yellow flower esteemed by the Virgin Mary. The plant is not a true marigold. True marigolds belong to the Aster Family. The genus name, *Caltha*, is derived from the Greek word *kalathos*, meaning "goblet." The species name, *palustris*, is Latin meaning "of marshes or wet places." All parts of the mature plant are poisonous, but they are said to be distasteful to livestock because of the acrid juice. A related species, Mountain Marsh Marigold (*C. leptosepala*), occurs in wet habitats in the subalpine and alpine zones. It has white flowers.

Meadow Buttercup
Ranunculus acris

BUTTERCUP FAMILY

This species is a European import that has widely established itself in our area. It grows from fibrous roots, stands up to 80 cm tall, and may have multiple stems. The leaves are hairy, heart-shaped, and deeply lobed almost to the base. The flowers are glossy and yellow, and appear singly or in loose clusters atop hairy stalks.

The genus name, *Ranunculus*, is explained in the note on Creeping Buttercup (*R. cymbalaria*), shown on page 7. The species name, *acris*, refers to the acrid juice of the plant. As a general rule, Buttercups contain alkaloids, and some species are poisonous to livestock. In fact, some Native peoples rubbed projectile points with juices from Buttercups to make them poisonous. According to Irish folklore, a cow's milk production would be enhanced if its udder was massaged with Buttercups—a proposition that is probably specious at best.

Prickly-Pear Cactus
Opuntia polyacantha
CACTUS FAMILY

This easily recognized plant is prostrate and can form mats on dry, exposed slopes in eroded areas and badlands, often growing on sandy or rocky soil. The stems are flattened and covered with clusters of hard, sharp spines that have tufts of sharp bristles at the base. The flowers are large and showy, with numerous yellow petals that are waxy, and up to 5 cm long. There is a conspicuous large green stigma and numerous yellow or orange stamens inside the flower. The fruits are reddish, soft, spiny berries which are edible, and are often browsed by antelope.

The genus name, *Opuntia*, is derived from the Greek name of a different plant that grew in Greece. The species name, *polyacantha*, is derived from the Greek *poly*, which means "many," and *acantha*, which means "thorns." Native peoples roasted and ate the plant stems, after removing the spines and outer skin. The juices inside the stem were often used as an emergency water supply. The plant contains calcium, phosphorus, and vitamin C, and is said to taste of cucumber. Brittle Prickly-Pear (*O. fragilis*) is a closely related species that occurs in the Peace River country of Alberta. It has round, rather than flat, joints between the stems.

Heart-Leaved Alexanders (Meadow Parsnip)
Zizia aptera
CARROT FAMILY

This is a plant of prairies, moist meadows, open woods, stream banks, and wetland margins. The small bright yellow flowers are numerous, and occur in compound, flat-topped clusters at the top of the stems. The lower leaves are leathery, dark green, and heart-shaped. The stem leaves are smaller and divided into 3 leaflets. The stem leaves become progressively smaller along the stem until they become cleft leaflets. The flowers appear on top of hollow stems that are erect, and reach heights of up to 60 cm.

The origin of the name Alexanders is unknown. The genus name, *Zizia*, honours an early German botanist, Johann Baptist Ziz. The species name, *aptera*, means "wingless," probably a reference to the shape of the fruit of the plant.

Leafy Musineon
Musineon divaricatum

CARROT FAMILY

This plant is a spreading or erect, low-growing perennial that grows up to 20 cm tall, from a thick, swollen taproot, and occurs in dry grasslands, exposed hillsides, and slopes with southerly or westerly exposures. The leaves are bright green and look like parsley, with many dissected leaflets. The flowers are yellow with 5 rounded petals, and occur in compact umbels atop the rough, glandular flower stalk. A number of such umbels can be found on each plant.

The genus name, *Musineon*, is the Greek name for some member of the Carrot Family in the Old World. The species name, *divaricatum*, probably refers to the divergent rays of the flower clusters.

Snakeroot
Sanicula marilandica
CARROT FAMILY

This erect perennial plant grows up to 100 cm tall from thick rootstock, and inhabits moist woods, shady aspen groves, and damp areas near waterways. The basal leaves are long-stalked and palmately divided into 5–7 leaflets (usually 5). The leaves are generally lance-shaped, with sharply toothed edges. The stem leaves are short-stalked or stalkless. The flowers appear in round clusters and can be yellowish, greenish-white, or white in colour.

The genus name, *Sanicula*, is derived from the Latin *sanare*, which means "to heal," it being believed that the plant had medicinal qualities. The species name is a reference to the State of Maryland, the plant being well distributed in much of the North American continent. The common name, Snakeroot, arises from a practice by Native peoples of using the plant in poultices to treat snakebite. The plant is also known by the common names Black Snakeroot, Black Sanicle, and Maryland Sanicle. This plant should not be confused with Seneca Snakeroot (*Polygala senega*), shown on page 161.

Annual Hawk's-Beard
Crepis tectorum
COMPOSITE FAMILY

A plant of moist open areas and saline meadows, this one- to three-stemmed annual will grow up to a metre in height. The basal leaves usually wither before flowering occurs. The stems have a few thin alternate leaves. Each plant will produce a few to 15 yellow flowers, composed of yellow ray flowers and no disk flowers. The fruits of the plant are dark purplish-brown achenes, with a pappus of fine, white, hair-like bristles at the top.

The genus name, *Crepis*, is derived from the Greek *krepis*, meaning "boot" or "sandal," and it may be a reference to the deeply cut leaves of some members of the genus, which may suggest the thongs of a sandal. The name Hawk's-Beard was given to the genus *Crepis* by the botanist Asa Grey, and it might refer to the pappus' resemblance to the bristly feathers that surround a hawk's beak.

Arrow-Leaved Balsamroot
Balsomorhiza sagittata

COMPOSITE FAMILY

A widespread and frequently abundant plant of hot, arid climates, often found on rocky south-facing slopes. The flowers are solitary composite heads with bright yellow ray flowers and yellow disk flowers, densely hairy, especially at the base. The leaves are large, arrowhead-shaped, silvery in colour, and covered by dense, felt-like hairs.

Also known as Oregon Sunflowers, the Balsamroot often provides a showy, early spring splash of colour on warm, dry hillsides. All parts of the plant are edible and provided an important food source for Native peoples. Some tribes smoked the leaves like tobacco. The seeds are similar to sunflower seeds, and were often dried and ground for use as flour. Deer and elk commonly browse on the plants. The genus name, *Balsomorhiza*, is from the Greek *balsamon*, meaning "balsam," and *rhiza*, meaning "root," a reference to the aromatic resin of the taproot. The species name, *sagittata*, is a reference to the arrowhead shape of the leaves.

Black-Eyed Susan
Rudbeckia hirta
COMPOSITE FAMILY

Colin Ladyka image

This introduced biennial or short-lived perennial grows up to 100 cm tall in meadows, disturbed areas, and along roadsides. The plant is rough-hairy throughout, and has purplish or reddish, simple to branched stems. The leaves are alternate and hairy. The lower leaves are elliptic, sometimes slightly toothed, and long-stalked. The upper leaves are narrow, lance-shaped, and short-stalked or sessile. The flower heads appear at the top of long stalks, and consist of 8–20 bright yellow to orange ray florets, surrounding a cone of dark purple to brown disk florets. The involucral bracts are hairy and slenderly pointed, becoming reflexed as the flower head matures. These reflexed bracts are probably the origin of the locally common name, Coneflower.

The genus name, *Rudbeckia*, honours Olaf Rudbeck, a professor of botany at the University of Uppsala, Sweden, who was an early benefactor of Carolus Linnaeus, the originator of binomial nomenclature for plants. Apparently, Professor Rudbeck took in the impoverished student Linnaeus and set him upon his illustrious career. The species name, *hirta*, means "hairy," a reference to the overall hairiness of the plant. This flower resembles Brown-Eyed Susan (*Gaillardia aristata*), shown on page 18. Brown-Eyed Susan has ray flowers that are usually red to purplish at the base, deeply three-lobed at the tip, and has a disk that is decidedly hairy.

Broomweed (Snakeweed)
Gutierrezia sarothrae
COMPOSITE FAMILY

This low-growing, many-branched, tufted perennial grows from a woody taproot to heights of 40 cm in dry grasslands, gravelly soil, and exposed slopes in badlands. The leaves are grey-green, slightly hairy, narrow, clasping on the stem, and dotted with glands. The yellow flowers are small and occur in numerous flat-topped to rounded heads at the top of the stems. The ray florets are few, and surround yellow disk florets. The bracts are sticky and glandular, with the lower bracts being greenish, and the upper bracts straw-coloured.

The genus name, *Gutierrezia*, honours Piedro Gutierrez, an early Spanish botanist. The species name, *sarothrae*, is derived from the Latin *sarotron*, which means "broom," most likely a reference to the twigs on the plant. This reference probably gives rise to the common name. The plant contains saponins, and is toxic to ungulates, cattle, and sheep. There is also some suspicion that the plant is a selenium concentrator. A tea made from the plant was used to treat snakebite, and that is probably the source of the common name Snakeweed. Other common names applied to the plant include Matchweed, Turpentine Weed, and Yellowtop.

Brown-Eyed Susan
Gaillardia aristata

COMPOSITE FAMILY

A plant of open grasslands, dry hillsides, roadsides, and open woods. The flowers are large and showy, with yellow ray florets that are purplish to reddish at the base. The central disk is purplish and woolly hairy. The leaves are numerous, alternate, and lance-shaped, usually looking greyish and rough, owing to the many short hairs.

The plant is named after a French botanist, Gaillard de Marentonneau. The species name, *aristata*, means "bristly" or "bearded," a reference to the bristles on the flower head. A number of Native peoples used the plant to relieve a variety of ailments, from menstrual problems, to gastroenteritis, to venereal disease, to saddle sores on horses. This flower is also commonly known as Blanketflower. The plant was first named and described by Frederick Pursh in 1814, from a specimen collected by Meriwether Lewis in 1806.

Colorado Rubber Weed
Hymenoxys richardsonii

COMPOSITE FAMILY

Glen Lee image

This perennial grows up to 30 cm tall from a woody rootstock, and occurs on dry, rocky, or eroded slopes, in grasslands, by roadsides, and in badlands. The leaves are mostly basal, alternate, smooth, have glandular dots, and are divided into 3–7 narrow, rubbery, wire-like segments. The flowers have few yellow ray florets that are three-lobed at the tip, and have yellow disk florets. The flower heads are borne at the ends of branches in a flat-topped cluster.

The origin of the genus name, *Hymenoxys*, is explained in the note on Stemless Rubber Weed (*H. acaulis*), shown on page 37. The species name honours explorer John Richardson, surgeon and naturalist, who served on two Arctic expeditions with Sir John Franklin. Stemless Rubber Weed is also in the same genus and occurs in the same habitat. The chief difference between the two plants is the leaves. In Stemless Rubber Weed the leaves are all basal and are covered in fine, silvery hairs, while in Colorado Rubber Weed the leaves are divided into narrow, rubbery, smooth segments.

Common Tansy
Tanacetum vulgare
COMPOSITE FAMILY

Anne Elliott image

This plant was introduced from Europe and is common along roadsides, embankments, pastures, fencerows, and disturbed areas. The flowers are yellow and occur in numerous bunches atop multiple stalks. They are flattened and resemble yellow buttons. The leaves are fern-like, dark green, finely dissected, and strong smelling.

Tansies are also known as Button Flowers. The genus name, *Tanacetum*, is derived from the Greek word *athanatos*, meaning "long-lasting," possibly a reference to the long-lasting flowers. In medieval England the plant was placed in shrouds to repel insects and rodents from corpses. It was originally cultivated in North America for its medicinal properties, and it spread from those cultivations. During the Middle Ages a posy of Tansies was thought to ward off the Black Death.

Dandelion
Taraxacum officinale

COMPOSITE FAMILY

This common, introduced plant is found in a variety of habitats the world over, and it is probably the most recognizable flower in our area for most people. The bright yellow flowers have ray florets only, and appear at the top of a smooth stem that arises from a whorl of basal leaves that are lance- to spoon-shaped and deeply incised. The flowers appear from early in the spring until late in the fall, giving this plant undoubtedly the longest blooming time of any flower in our area.

Though everybody seems to recognize this flower, it is interesting to note that more than 1,000 kinds of Dandelions have been described. The common name for this plant is thought to be a corruption of the French *le dent-de-lion*, meaning "the tooth of the lion," a reference to the shape of the leaf. All parts of the plant are edible—the young leaves are eaten raw or cooked as greens, the roots are dried and ground as a coffee substitute, and the flowers can be used to make wine. Some people roll the flower heads in flour and deep-fry them, claiming they have a flavour similar to morel mushrooms when so prepared. The sap from the plant was used in Ireland to treat warts.

Goat's-Beard
Tragopogon dubius
COMPOSITE FAMILY

A plant of the grasslands, roadsides, ditches, and dry waste areas. Goat's-Beard was introduced from Europe and is also known as Yellow Salsify. The flower is a large solitary, erect yellow head, surrounded by long, narrow green protruding bracts. The leaves are alternate, fleshy, and narrow, but broad and clasping at the base. The fruit is a mass of white narrow, ribbed, beaked achenes that resembles the seed pod of a common dandelion, but is significantly larger—approaching the size of a softball.

The flowers open on sunny mornings, but then close up around noon and stay closed for the rest of the day. They usually will not open on cloudy or rainy days. The common name, Goat's-Beard, is probably a reference to the mass of white achenes, which is said to resemble a goat's beard. The genus name, *Tragopogon* is derived from the Greek *tragos*, meaning "goat," and *pogon*, meaning "beard." The young leaves and roots from immature plants may be eaten. The leaves and stems exude a milky, latex-like juice when cut, which may be chewed like gum when hardened. A similar species, Purple Salsify or Oyster Plant (*T. porrifolius*) appears in the same habitat, but has a purple flower.

Gumweed
Grindelia squarrosa
COMPOSITE FAMILY

Anne Elliott image

This plant is a sticky perennial or biennial that grows to heights of 100 cm from a deep taproot, and occurs on roadsides, saline flats, slough margins, riverflats, and dry grasslands. Its leaves are dark green, narrowly oblong, entire or slightly toothed, and glandular-sticky. The lower leaves have long stalks, while the upper ones are stalkless and somewhat clasping, with pointed or rounded tips. The flowers appear as numerous heads, with bright yellow ray florets up to 15 cm long, tapering from the middle to each end. The disk florets are yellow, dense, and up to 2 cm across. The involucral bracts are numerous, sticky, shiny, narrow, overlapping, and sometimes reflexed.

The genus name, *Grindelia*, honours David Grindel, a 19th-century Russian botanist. The species name, *squarrosa*, means "with parts spreading or recurved at the ends," a reference to the reflexed bracts. The common name, Gumweed, alludes to the sticky resins produced by the plant. The plant contains resins, tannic acid, volatile oils, and an alkaloid. Research discloses that it was viewed as a cornucopia of pharmacology by Native peoples and early settlers, being variously used to treat poison ivy, bronchitis, asthma, pneumonia, colds, muscle spasms, coughs, liver problems, kidney disease, syphilis, and as a contraceptive. It was also employed as a veterinary medicine for horses. The plant has a number of locally common names, including Resin Weed, Gum Plant, Tarweed, Curly-Cup Gumweed, and Curly-Top Gumweed.

Hairy Golden Aster
Heterotheca villosa
COMPOSITE FAMILY

This is a plant of dry, open, sandy prairie and hillsides, particularly where there are southerly exposures. The bright yellow flowers appear in numbers, with bright yellow ray florets and yellow to brown disk florets. The leaves are oblong, and more or less hairy.

At one time this plant had the scientific name *Chrysopsis villosa. Chrysopsis* is derived from the Greek *chrysos*, meaning "gold," and *opsis*, meaning "aspect"—thus Golden Aster. The species name, *villosa*, means "hairy," and is a reference to the overall hairiness of the plant.

Heart-Leafed Arnica
Arnica cordifolia

COMPOSITE FAMILY

Arnica is a common plant of wooded areas in the Rocky Mountains, foothills, and boreal forest. The leaves occur in 2–4 opposite pairs along the stem, each with long stalks and heart-shaped, serrated blades. The uppermost pair is stalkless and more lance-shaped than the lower leaves. The flowers have 10–15 bright yellow ray florets, and bright yellow central disk florets.

Without careful dissection of the plant and examination under magnification, recognition of specific members of the Arnica Family can be difficult. The leaf structure on an individual plant is often the best clue to species recognition. The genus name, *Arnica*, is derived from the Greek *arnakis*, meaning "lamb's skin," a reference to the woolly bracts and leaf texture on many members of the genus. The species name, *cordifolia*, means "heart-shaped," a reference to the leaves of the plant. This species occasionally hybridizes with Mountain Arnica (*A. latifolia*) and the resulting hybrid can be difficult to identify. A number of Native peoples used Arnicas as a poultice for swellings and bruises. Arnicas are said to be poisonous if ingested.

Late Goldenrod
Solidago gigantea

COMPOSITE FAMILY

A plant of moist woods and meadows, floodplains, and lake shores. The flowers are bright yellow, terminal, broadly pyramidal clusters of flower heads. The leaves are numerous, alternate, thin and lance-shaped, usually smooth, toothed from above the middle, and tapering to the base.

The genus name, *Solidago*, is probably derived from the Latin *solidus*, meaning "whole," and *ago*, meaning "to do or make," a reference to the plant's healing properties. The species name, *gigantea*, means "large." The word "late" in the common name refers to the late flowering of the plant. This species is very similar to Canada Goldenrod (*S. canadensis*), but that species has leaves that are hairy, and stems that are hairy above the middle. Velvety Goldenrod (*S. mollis*), is also similar, but it has grey-green, velvety-hairy, broadly lance-shaped leaves, the uppermost of which exhibit 3 distinct veins. Velvety Goldenrod is usually found in the southern extremities of the area. Stiff Goldenrod (*S. rigida*) is also found in the area, but its flower clusters are most often flat-topped, not pyramid-shaped. Some Native peoples ground the flowers of Goldenrods into a lotion and applied it to bee stings.

Marsh Ragwort
Senecio congestus
COMPOSITE FAMILY

Colin Ladyka image

Of all of the species of Ragwort (Groundsel) found in the area, this one is probably the most distinctive. It is tall, very leafy, densely soft-haired, and prefers moist, wet, marshy places. These plants can occur in profusion around marshes, ponds and sloughs. The plant can reach 80 cm in height, and its basal leaves are up to 15 cm long, lance- to spatula-shaped, with wavy margins. The upper stem leaves are shorter and clasping. The inflorescence has several to many flower heads in a dense, branched cluster, with each head consisting of small, bright yellow flowers composed of ray florets and disk florets.

The origin of the genus name, *Senecio*, is explained in the note on Prairie Groundsel (*S. canus*), shown on page 32. All members of the genus contain toxic alkaloids. Ragwort and Groundsel seem to be interchangeable names for members of the genus. Indeed, a locally common name for this plant is Northern Swamp Groundsel

Narrow-Leaved Hawkweed
Hieracium umbellatum

COMPOSITE FAMILY

A plant common to open woods, meadows, roadsides, ditches, and disturbed areas, growing to heights of up to 100 cm. The yellow flower heads appear in a cluster on ascending stalks from a usually solitary, hairy stem. The flowers are composed entirely of ray florets, with no disk florets. The basal and lower stem leaves usually fall off before flowering occurs. The upper stem leaves are lance-shaped and usually stalkless (sessile).

The genus name *Hieracium* is derived from the Greek *hierax*, meaning "hawk," as it was once believed that eating these plants improved a hawk's vision. Why such a belief once prevailed is a complete mystery. The species name, *umbellatum*, is likely a reference to the umbel-like flower arrangement. The leaves, stems, and roots produce a milky latex that was used as a chewing gum by some Native peoples. A similar species, Slender Hawkweed (*H. gracile*) occurs in subalpine and alpine habitat, but it is very much shorter overall. White Hawkweed (*H. albiflorum*) has a white flower, and occurs in similar habitat to Narrow-Leaved Hawkweed.

Nodding Beggarticks
Bidens cernua

COMPOSITE FAMILY

Glen Lee image

This plant is an annual, erect, branching, leafy species that grows to heights of 70 cm or more, and occurs in the edges of sloughs, ponds, slow-moving streams, ditches and marshes. The leaves are opposite, stalkless, narrowly lance-shaped, with wavy or coarsely toothed margins. The stems on the plant are smooth. The yellow flowers are nodding and occur in bristly flower heads. The flowers often have a ragged conformation, with the yellow ray flowers unevenly spaced, or even missing, as they surround the yellow and black disk flowers. The fruits are dry, barbed achenes, which often catch on the fur of passing animals or the clothing of passing humans.

The genus name, *Bidens*, is derived from Latin and means "two teeth," a reference to the double awns of some species in the genus. The species name comes from the Latin *cernuum*, which means "nodding" or "drooping," a reference to the nodding flower heads. The common name Beggarticks arises because of the prickly, barbed fruits of the plant.

Perennial Sow-Thistle
Sonchus arvensis
COMPOSITE FAMILY

A plant of cultivated fields, roadsides, ditches, and pastures. The flowers have large, yellow ray florets similar to dandelion flowers. Sow-Thistle is an imported species from Europe. It is not a true thistle. Sow-Thistles will exude a milky latex when the stem is crushed. True thistles do not do so.

The common name is derived from the fact that pigs like to eat this plant. The genus name, *Sonchus*, is derived from the Greek word *somphos*, meaning "spongy," a reference to the stems. The species name, *arvensis*, means "of the fields," a reference to the fact that the plant often invades cultivated ground.

Prairie Coneflower
Ratibida columnifera

COMPOSITE FAMILY

This is a plant of dry grasslands, coulees, and disturbed areas, and can reach heights of up to 60 cm. The leaves are alternate, greyish-green in colour, and deeply divided into oblong lobes. The distinctive flower appears atop a tall, slender stem, and consists of dark purple disk florets formed into a cylinder up to 4 cm long, the base of which is surrounded by bright yellow petals.

The origin of the genus name, *Ratibida*, is unknown. The species name, *columnifera*, is a reference to the column- or cone-shaped flower. Some Native peoples dried the flowers for food, while others made a tea from the disk florets and leaves. The roots of the plant yield a yellow dye. Another similar plant is Purple Coneflower (*Echinacea angustifolia*), which has brownish-red disk flowers surrounded by reflexed light purple or lavender ray flowers. It is a popular garden ornamental, but is relatively rare on the prairies.

Prairie Groundsel (Woolly Groundsel)
Senecio canus

COMPOSITE FAMILY

This is a white, woolly perennial that can stand up to 40 cm in height.
It occurs at a variety of elevations, from prairie to almost timberline.
The leaves are clustered at the base, with taller stems supporting the flowers.
Stem leaves are alternate and reduced in size as the stem rises. All leaves are
greyish-green and covered with white, fuzzy hairs. The yellow flower heads
are solitary to several on a stem, with notched ray florets surrounding a
cluster of disk florets.

The genus name, *Senecio*, is derived from the Latin *senex*, meaning "old
man," and may be a reference to the grey, beard-like hair that covers the
plant. The species name, *canus*, means "ash coloured," and refers to the
leaves. The Groundsels contain toxic alkaloids. Other common names
applied to plants in this genus include Butterweed and Ragwort.

Prairie Sunflower
Helianthus annuus
COMPOSITE FAMILY

For many people, this may be one of the most recognizable flowers on the prairies. It is a bushy, robust, rough-hairy annual that grows on stout stems to over a metre tall along roadsides, meadows, marshes, and dry, eroded slopes. The large leaves are mostly alternate, prominently veined, have a hairy, rough surface, and are usually toothed. The lower leaves are heart-shaped, while the upper leaves are somewhat triangular. The flowers are large and showy, with bright yellow, pointed, grooved, ray florets up to 5 cm long, and reddish-brown to purple disk florets.

The genus name, *Helianthus*, is derived from the Greek *helios*, meaning "sun," and *anthos*, meaning "flower." Some Native peoples ate the seeds of the plant, either raw or cooked. The seeds have also been used medicinally to treat respiratory diseases and whooping cough. They have also been roasted and ground as a coffee substitute, and dried as a tobacco substitute. Rhombic-Leaved Sunflower (*H. rigidus*) is a similar related Sunflower that occurs in the same habitat. Its leaves are rhomboid—diamond-shaped.

Shining Arnica (Orange Arnica)
Arnica fulgens

COMPOSITE FAMILY

A plant of moist grasslands to low elevations in the mountains, this Arnica grows up to 60 cm in height. The leaves are greyish-green and mostly basal, opposite, lance-shaped, stalked, and tapering to the base. There are small tufts of brown hairs between the basal leaf stalks and stem. The paired stem leaves are smaller than the basal leaves, stalkless or nearly so, and lance-shaped to linear. The flower heads are usually solitary with yellow ray florets surrounding yellow disk florets that exhibit spreading white hairs.

For an explanation of the genus name, see Heart-Leafed Arnica (*A. cordifolia*), shown on page 25. The species name, *fulgens,* means "shining," and is said to be a reference to the bright flowers against the greyish-green background of the plant's leaves. This species occasionally hybridizes with Mountain Arnica (*A. latifolia*), and the resulting hybrid can be difficult to identify. A number of Native peoples used Arnicas as a poultice for swellings and bruises. Arnicas are said to be poisonous if ingested.

Short-Beaked Agoseris (False Dandelion)
Agoseris glauca
COMPOSITE FAMILY

A plant common to moist to dry openings, meadows, and dry open forests. This plant is also known as False Dandelion. The Agoseris shares many characteristics with the Dandelions, including a long taproot, a rosette of basal leaves, a leafless stem, a single yellow flower appearing on a long stalk, and the production of a sticky, milky juice which is apparent when the stem is broken. In fact, this flower is often passed over as just another Dandelion, but upon closer examination several differences are apparent. Agoseris is generally a taller plant than Dandelion, its leaves are longer, and the leaf blades are smooth or faintly toothed, rather than deeply incised. The bracts of the Agoseris flower heads are broader than Dandelions, and are never turned back along the stem, as they are in Dandelions.

Some Native peoples used the milky juice of the plant as a chewing gum. Infusions from the plant were also used for a variety of medicinal purposes. Agoseris also appears in an orange form (*A. aurantiaca*) that inhabits the same environment, often at higher elevations.

Sneezeweed
Helenium autumnale

COMPOSITE FAMILY

Glen Lee image

This sparsely hairy to smooth glandular perennial grows up to 150 cm tall from fibrous roots, and occurs in wet locations, such as stream banks, ditches, and slough margins. The numerous leaves are glandular-dotted, hairy, shallowly toothed or entire, lance-shaped to oval, and up to 15 cm long. The leaves are alternate, stalkless for the most part, and decurrent—extending down from the point of insertion—so when the edges of the leaves continue down the stem, they form wings on the stem. The flowers occur in heads at the ends of the branches, with up to 20 yellow ray florets that are wedge-shaped, often bend downward, and three-lobed at the tip. The disk florets are yellow and glandular, and occur in a round disk up to 2 cm across.

The genus name, *Helenium*, is to honour Helen of Troy. Legend has it that when she wept for the lives lost by her would-be rescuers, these flowers sprang from the ground where her tears fell. The species name, *autumnale*, means "pertaining to autumn," and is a reference to the late blooming habit of these plants. The common name, Sneezeweed, is said to come from the practice of some Native peoples of drying the plant and using it as snuff. The plant is said to be poisonous to livestock, but most often livestock ignore it.

Stemless Rubber Weed (Butte Marigold)
Hymenoxys acaulis

COMPOSITE FAMILY

This creeping, tufted, hairy perennial grows up to 30 cm tall from a woody rootstock, and often forms small colonies. It occurs on dry, rocky, or sandy exposed slopes, in grasslands, by roadsides, and in badlands. The leaves are all basal, entire, narrowly lance-shaped to spoon-shaped, and softly hairy. The flowers are bright yellow, solitary heads that are borne on leafless stalks. The ray flowers are yellow, three-lobed at the tip, and reflex with age. The disk flowers are yellow or orange-yellow. The involucral bracts are white, hairy, linear, and not united at the base.

The origin of the genus name, *Hymenoxys*, is derived from the Greek *hymen*, meaning "membrane," and *oxys*, meaning "sharp," a reference to the scales on the pappus of the fruit of the plant. The roots of plants in this genus exude a white sap when cut or crushed, and that is most likely the origin of the common name Rubber Weed. Colorado Rubber Weed (*H. richardsonii*), shown on page 19, is in the same genus and occurs in the same habitat.

Yellow Evening-Primrose
Oenothera biennis

EVENING PRIMROSE FAMILY

An erect, robust, leafy biennial, this plant forms a rosette of leaves the first year, and puts up a tall, leafy stem the second. The flowers have large, bright yellow, cross-shaped stigma, with numerous yellow stamens. The flowers usually open in the evening and fade in the morning.

The plant gets its common name by its habit of blooming at dusk to attract moths for pollination. The genus name, *Oenothera* is derived from the Greek word meaning "wine scented"—*oinos* meaning "wine," and *thera* meaning "to induce wine drinking." The name is said to arise because an allied European plant was thought to induce a taste for wine. The roots of the first-year plant were often dug and boiled for food, or were dried for later use. They are said to be nutritious and have a nut-like flavour. Seed oil from the plant is used for medicinal purposes. Another member of the genus, White Evening-Primrose (*O. nuttallii*) is found in the area in dry, sandy habitat. It has white (sometimes pinkish) flowers and white, shredding stems.

Butter and Eggs
Linaria vulgaris

FIGWORT FAMILY

Anne Elliott image

A common plant of roadsides, ditches, fields, and disturbed areas, which reaches heights of up to a metre. Also known as Toadflax. The leaves are alternate, dark green, and narrow. The flowers are similar in shape to Snapdragons. The bright yellow flowers with orange throats occur in dense, terminal clusters at the tops of erect stems. The corolla is spurred at the base and two-lipped; the upper lip two-lobed, and the lower lip three-lobed.

The flower takes its common name, Butter and Eggs, from the yellow and orange tones that resemble the colour of butter and eggs. There are two schools of thought as to the origin of the other common name, Toadflax. In early English, "toad" meant "false" or "useless," ergo "useless flax" or "false flax"—the leaves of this plant resembling those of Flax. The other school of thought attributes the name "toad" to the resemblance of the flower to that of a toad's mouth. Toadflax was introduced to North America from Europe as a garden plant, but escapees from the garden have become noxious weeds. It was used in early Europe to treat jaundice, piles, and eye infections, and was also boiled in milk to make a fly poison. The genus name, *Linaria*, refers to the general similarity of the leaves of this plant to those of Flax. Dalmatian Toadflax (*L. dalmatica*) is a similar species that appears in the same habitat. It has clasping, broadly oval leaves, and larger flowers.

Common Mullein
Verbascum thapsis

FIGWORT FAMILY

A Eurasian import that grows up to 2 m tall, Mullein is quite common along roadsides, gravelly places and dry slopes. The plant is a biennial, taking 2 years to produce flowers. In the first year the plant puts out a rosette of large leaves which are very soft to the touch, much like velvet or flannel. From those leaves surges the strong sentinel-like stalk in the second year. The small yellow flowers appear randomly from a flowering spike atop the stalk. It appears that at no time do all the flowers bloom together. After flowering, the dead stalk turns to a dark brown colour, and the stalk may persist for many months.

A common name for the plant is Flannel Mullein, a reference to the soft texture of the basal leaves. Mullein is derived from the Latin *mollis*, which means "soft." The dried leaves of the plant were sometimes smoked by Native peoples, and the plant is also sometimes called Indian Tobacco. The crushed leaves were often used as a poultice applied to swelling and wounds because the chemicals in the plant soothe irritated tissues and act as a sedative.

Yellow Beardtongue
Penstemon confertus

FIGWORT FAMILY

This is a plant of moist to dry meadows, woodlands, stream banks, hillsides and mountains, and occurs from the prairie to the alpine zone. The small pale yellow flowers are numerous, and appear in whorled, interrupted clusters along the upper part of the stem. Each flower is tube shaped, and has 2 lips. The lower lip is three-lobed and bearded at the throat; the upper lip is two-lobed.

The origin of the common name, Beardtongue, and the genus name, *Penstemon*, is explained in the narrative on Lilac-Flowered Beardtongue (*P. gracilis*), shown on page 84. The species name, *confertus*, is Latin, meaning "crowded," a reference to the numerous flowers in the clusters. A number of Penstemons appear in Western Canada.

Yellow Monkeyflower
Mimulus guttatus

FIGWORT FAMILY

This plant occurs, often in large patches, along streams, seeps, and in moist meadows. The plant is quite variable, but always spectacular when found. The bright yellow flowers resemble Snapdragons, and occur in clusters. The flowers usually have red or purple dots on the lip, giving the appearance of a grinning face.

The genus name, *Mimulus*, is derived from the Latin *mimus*, meaning "mimic" or "actor," a reference to the "face" seen on the flower. The species name, *guttatus*, means "spotted" or "speckled." A related species, Red Monkeyflower (*M. lewisii*), is named in honour of Meriwether Lewis of the Lewis and Clark expedition, who collected the first specimen of the plant in 1805 near the headwaters of the Missouri River in Montana.

Golden Corydalis
Corydalis aurea

FUMITORY FAMILY

This plant of open woods, roadsides, disturbed places, and stream banks is an erect or spreading, branched, leafy biennial or annual. It germinates in the fall and overwinters as a seedling. In the spring, it grows rapidly, flowers, and then dies. The yellow flowers are irregularly shaped, rather like the flowers of the Pea Family, with keels at the tips. A long, nectar-producing spur extends backwards from the upper petal.

The genus name, *Corydalis*, is derived from the Greek *korydallis*, meaning "crested lark," a reference to the spur of the petal resembling the spur of a lark. The species name, *aurea*, means "golden." Corydalis is generally considered poisonous because it contains isoquinoline and other alkaloids. Some poisoning of livestock has been reported. A similar species, Pink Corydalis (*C. sempervirens*), appears in similar habitat, but it has pink flowers with yellow tips, and is a taller and more erect plant.

Twining Honeysuckle
Lonicera dioica var. *glaucescens*

HONEYSUCKLE FAMILY

A flowering vine, this plant clambers over low bushes and shrubs, and around tree trunks, at low to subalpine elevations. The trumpet-shaped flowers cluster inside a shallow cup formed by 2 leaves that are joined at their bases. The cupped leaves are very distinctive. When the flowers first open, they are yellow, turning orange to brick colour with age. The 5 petals are united into a funnel-shaped tube that has a swollen knob near the base where nectar is accumulated. Insects puncture the knob to obtain the sweet nectar. The flowers are very sweet scented. The fruits are small red berries, appearing in clusters.

The genus name, *Lonicera*, is to honour a 16th-century German botanist and physician, Adam Lonitzer. The common name, Honeysuckle, describes the sweet-tasting nectar of the flower. The stems of the Honeysuckle were woven into mats, bags, and blankets by various Native tribes.

Yellowbell
Fritillaria pudica

LILY FAMILY

This diminutive flower is a harbinger of spring, blooming often just after snowmelt in dry grasslands and dry open Ponderosa pine forests. It can easily be overlooked because of its small size, usually standing only about 15 cm tall. The yellow, drooping, bell-shaped flowers are very distinctive. The flowers turn orange to brick-red as they age. The leaves (usually 2 or 3) are linear to lance-shaped, and appear more or less opposite about halfway up the stem. The Yellowbell sometimes appears with 2 flowers on a stem, but single blooms are more common.

The genus name *Fritillaria* is derived from the Latin *fritillus*, "a dice box," probably a reference to the fruit, which appears as an erect, cylindrical capsule. The species name *pudica* means "bashful," and is probably a reference to the nodding attitude of the flower on the stem. Native peoples gathered the bulbs and used them as a food source, eating them both raw and cooked.

Prairie Rocket
Erysimum asperum

MUSTARD FAMILY

Prairie Rocket grows in dry, sandy grasslands. This erect, robust plant can reach heights approaching a metre. The bright yellow flowers grow at the terminal ends of stout branching stems, and appear in rounded clusters. The stem leaves on the plant are simple, alternate, and lance-shaped.

The genus name, *Erysimum*, is derived from the Greek *erysio*, meaning "to draw out," a reference to the acrid juices of such plants being used in poultices. The species name, *asperum*, means "rough" a likely reference to the stiff hairs found on the plant. At one time, children were treated for worms with a concoction made up of the crushed seeds of this plant mixed in water.

Sand Bladderpod
Lesquerella arenosa

MUSTARD FAMILY

This grey-coloured annual is a short, tufted, spreading plant that grows several stems from a taproot. The leaves are mainly in a basal rosette. The basal leaves are linear to spoon-shaped, gradually tapering to the base, are hairy with star-shaped hairs, and up to 8 cm long. The stem leaves that support the flowers radiate from the basal leaves like spokes in a wheel. The numerous, small, yellow flowers have 4 petals, typical of mustards, and occur in loose, open clusters at the top of the stems.

The genus name, *Lesquerella*, honours Leo Lesquereux, (pronounced "le crew"), a 19th-century Swiss-born American naturalist and paleontologist, who is considered by many to be America's first paleobotanist. The species name, *arenosa*, means "of sand or sandy places," a reference to the growth habitat of the plant. The common name, Bladderpod, is derived from the fruits of the plant, which are round, grey-green, hairy pods characteristic of the Mustard Family.

Soopolallie (Canadian Buffaloberry)
Shepherdia canadensis

OLEASTER FAMILY

This deciduous shrub grows up to 3 m tall, and is often the dominant understory cover in lodgepole pine forests. All parts of the plant are covered with rust-coloured, shiny scales, giving the whole plant an orange, rusty appearance. The leaves are leathery and thick, green and glossy on the upper surface, while the lower surface is covered with white hairs and sprinkled with rusty coloured dots. The plant is dioecious; that is, the male and female flowers appear on separate plants. The small inconspicuous yellow flowers often appear on the branches of the plant prior to the arrival of the leaves. The male flowers have 4 stamens, while the female flowers have none. In the fall, the female shrubs will be covered with small, translucent berries that are predominantly red.

The genus name, *Shepherdia*, is to honour the 18th-century English botanist, John Shepherd. The common name, Soopolallie, is from the Chinook tribe—*soop*, meaning "soap," and *olallie*, meaning "berry"—a reference to the fact that when beaten in water, the red berries produce a pink, soapy froth that some Native peoples liked to drink. The foam is derived from the bitter chemical saponins contained in the berries. Bears seem to relish the berries, and early settlers reported that buffalo browsed them, thus two of the common names. Other common names for the plant include Soapberry, Russet Buffaloberry, and Bearberry.

Wolf Willow (Silverberry)
Elaeagnus commutata

OLEASTER FAMILY

This deciduous shrub grows up to 4 m tall, and often occurs in dense stands. The twigs are densely covered with rusty brown scales, and the leaves are alternate, oval, silvery in colour, and covered with small scales. The flowers are funnel-shaped and have 4 yellow lobes, occurring at the leaf axils. The flowers are very fragrant with a distinctive aroma. The fruits are silvery, round to egg-shaped berries, and usually persist throughout the winter.

The genus name, *Elaeagnus* is derived from the Greek *elaia*, meaning "olive," and *agnos*, meaning "willow." Native peoples used the tough, fibrous bark of the plant to make bags, baskets, and rope. The berries of the plant were often used as beads for personal adornment. A very similar plant, Russian Olive (*E. angustifolia*), was introduced from Europe and used as a windbreak, but it is a larger plant and has thorns.

Yellow Lady's Slipper
Cypripedium parviflorum (formerly *C. calceolus*)

ORCHID FAMILY

An orchid of bogs, damp woods, and stream banks. The leaves are alternate, with 2–4 per stem, broadly elliptic, and clasping. The yellow flowers usually occur 1 per stem, and resemble a small shoe. The sepals and lateral petals are similar, greenish-yellow to brownish, with twisted, wavy margins. The lower petal forms a prominent pouch-shaped yellow lip with purple dotting around the puckered opening.

The genus name, *Cypripedium*, is derived from *Cypris*, another name for Aphrodite, and *pedilon*, which means "foot." Yellow Lady's Slipper was originally known as *Calceolus mariae*, which translates into "St. Mary's little shoe." Bees enter the opening of the "slipper" and cannot exit without being covered in pollen. This lovely flower has suffered large range reductions as a result of picking and attempted transplantation, which almost always fails. There are several other Lady's Slippers that occur in the prairies, but are generally rare—Stemless Lady's Slipper (*C. acaule*) is predominantly pink; Ram's Head Lady's Slipper (*C. arietinum*) is greenish-purple; Showy Lady's Slipper (*C. reginae*) is pink with purple stripes; and Sparrow's-Egg Lady's Slipper (*C. passerinum*), shown on page 167, is white with purple spots.

Buffalo Bean (Golden Bean)
Thermopsis rhombifolia

PEA FAMILY

A plant of grassy hillsides, roadsides, ditches, and prairies, this member of the Pea Family can form large clumps from its creeping rootstock. The flower is bright yellow and blooms in crowded clusters atop the stem, which grows to 35 cm. The flower has the typical pea shape, with the keel enclosing the stamens. The leaves are opposite, alternate, compound, and clasping leaflets.

The genus name is derived from the Greek *thermos*, meaning "lupine," and *opsis*, meaning "resemblance," because the flowers are similar in shape to those of Lupines. The species name, *rhombifolia*, means "with rhombic (diamond-shaped) leaves." The plant takes its common name from Blackfoot parlance. The Blackfoot believed that when this flower bloomed, it was time to go hunting buffalo, the buffalo having had a chance to fatten on spring grasses. It was not eaten by buffalo because the plant contains poisonous alkaloids. Mountain Goldenpea (*T. montana*) is a similar species that appears in wet meadows at higher elevations. That species can grow up to a metre in height.

Caragana
Caragana arborescens
PEA FAMILY

This large deciduous shrub or small tree was introduced into the area from Siberia and Manchuria for use as hedges and windbreaks, and it has naturalized in the new environment exceedingly well. It is a multi-stemmed shrub with erect to spreading branches that grows up to 5 m tall. The leaves are alternate, pinnately compound with 8–12 oval, entire, tipped leaflets. The flowers are small, yellow and pea-like, occurring singly or in clusters. The twigs are green to grey-brown, and often have weak, paired spines at the nodes. The fruits are slender, cylindrical legume pods that are brown to tan in colour.

Caragana is particularly well adapted to prairie conditions in Canada. It is a very cold-tolerant plant, and does well in long, hot, dry summers, and cold, dry winters. It is also tolerant of very alkaline soils. The plant has a symbiotic relationship with certain soil bacteria, which form nodules on the roots and fix atmospheric nitrogen, which is taken up by the host plant and other adjacent plants.

Cushion Milk-Vetch
Astragalus triphyllus

PEA FAMILY

This low-growing species forms dense mats of leaves and flower stems on the ground, and occurs on dry slopes and hillsides in the prairies, in coulees, and on eroded ground. The leaves are compound, with 3 elliptic leaflets, and are thickly clustered around the base. The leaves and stems are densely covered with soft, silvery hairs, giving the plant a greyish-green hue. The flowers are yellowish-white (typical of the Pea Family), have a purplish tint on the keel, and occur in short-stemmed clusters that are somewhat buried in the leaves. The distinguishing feature of this species that sets it apart from other members of the genus is its three-parted leaves. All of the other members of the genus have pinnately compound leaves with numerous leaflets.

The origin of the genus name, *Astragalus*, is explained in the note on Two-Grooved Milk-Vetch (*A. bisulcatus*), shown on page 110. Plants of this genus might be confused with those of *Oxytropis*, the Locoweeds, in which the flowers are similar. However, the flowers of Locoweeds are usually on leafless stalks, and always have a pointed projection at the tip of the keel.

Field Locoweed
Oxytropis campestris

PEA FAMILY

This early-blooming plant is widespread and common in rocky outcrops, roadsides, and dry open woods in the region. The leaves are mainly basal, with elliptical leaflets and dense hairs. The pale yellow pea-like flowers bloom in clusters at the top of a leafless, hairy stem.

The genus name, *Oxytropis*, is derived from the Greek *oxys*, meaning "sharp" or "bitter," and *tropis*, meaning "keel," a reference to the sharp keel on the flower. The species name, *campestris*, means "field loving." The plant is poisonous to cattle, sheep, and horses, owing to its high content of alkaloids that cause blind staggers. This loss of muscle control in animals that have ingested the plant is the origin of the common name for the flower, *loco* being Spanish for "mad" or "foolish." Plants of this genus might be confused with those of *Astragalus*, the Milk-Vetches, in which the flowers are similar. However, the flowers of Locoweeds are usually on leafless stalks, and always have a pointed projection at the tip of the keel.

Yellow Hedysarum
Hedysarum sulphurescens

PEA FAMILY

A plant of stream banks, grasslands, open forests, and clearings. The flowers are pea-like, yellowish to nearly white, drooping, and appear usually along one side of the stem in elongated clusters (racemes). The fruits of the plant are long, flattened, pendulous pods, with conspicuous winged edges and constrictions between each of the seeds.

The genus name, *Hedysarum*, is derived from the Greek *hedys*, meaning "sweet," and *aroma*, meaning "smell." Yellow Hedysarum is also called Yellow Sweet Vetch. It is an extremely important food source for grizzly bears, which eat the roots in the spring and fall.

Yellow Sweet-Clover
Melilotus officinalis

PEA FAMILY

A plant of roadsides, ditches, embankments, and pastures, this introduced plant is quite common. It grows to over 2 m in height, with smooth, leafy, branched stems. The leaflets are slightly toothed, and appear in threes. The flowers are yellow, and appear in long, narrow, tapered clusters at the top of the plant and in the leaf axils. Each individual flower has a typical pea shape, with standard, wings, and a keel. In this flower the standard and wings are about the same length, and the wings are attached to the keel.

The genus name, *Melilotus*, is derived from the Greek *meli*, meaning "honey," and *lotos*, the name of some clover-like plant in the Mediterranean. *Officinalis* means "yellow." This plant, and a similar plant, White Sweet-Clover, (*M. alba*), were introduced as a forage plant for livestock. Both plants contain coumarin, which imparts an overwhelmingly sweet fragrance when you are near the plants, or when they are cut for hay.

Fringed Loosestrife
Lysimachia ciliata

PRIMROSE FAMILY

Anne Elliott image

This is an erect plant, growing up to 100 cm tall, that occurs in prairie to montane zones in woods, damp meadows, thickets, and on stream banks. The leaves are large, opposite, prominently veined, oval to broadly lance-shaped, rounded at the base, pointed at the end, and fringed with white hairs. The large yellow flowers appear from the upper leaf axils, and have 5 petals with fringed margins and reddish glandular bases. The tips of the petals are usually unevenly pointed.

The genus name, *Lysimachia*, is derived from the Greek *lysis*, which means "to release" or "loosening," and *mache*, which means "strife" or "battle." The exact taxonomic reference to this plant is unclear, but two stories are presented by the authorities as to the connection. The first holds that Pliny, a Roman historian, reported that Lysimachos, King of Thrace and companion of Alexander the Great, used the plant to calm an angry bull. The other story, similar in part, holds that Loosestrife deters flies and gnats, and was attached to the harnesses of draught animals to quiet them. Interestingly, it is also said that the plant was burned inside houses to repel snakes and insects.

Agrimony
Agrimonia striata
ROSE FAMILY

This erect, brownish-hairy perennial grows to over a metre tall and inhabits the open woods, often found growing in thickets, clearings, and along roadsides and trails. The leaves are pinnately divided into 7–11 lance-shaped, toothed, hairy major leaflets, with smaller ones often occurring between the major leaflets. The leaves are dark green and have tiny, stalkless glands beneath. The flowers are small, bright yellow, five-petaled, and occur in dense, long, narrow, interrupted clusters at the top of the stem. The fruits are dry, cup-shaped achenes, with hooked prickles that adhere to clothing of passersby and the fur of passing animals.

The genus name, *Agrimonia*, is said to be derived from the Greek *argema*, an eye disease that the plant was thought to cure. The species name, *striata*, means "scalloped." The plant was used medicinally to treat a variety of ailments, including diabetes, bladder afflictions, fever, jaundice, and tapeworms. Some people exhibit dermatological reactions like rashes or inflammations if they handle the plant. Other common names for the plant include Woodland Agrimony, Roadside Agrimony, Harvest-Lice, Snakeweed, and Sweethearts.

Early Cinquefoil
Potentilla concinna

ROSE FAMILY

A short, spreading perennial that supports 2–5 flowers per plant.
The flowers are bright yellow with 5 rounded petals appearing as solitary
flowers atop a leafless stem. The plant is usually less than 10 cm tall overall.

The Early Cinquefoil appears early in the spring and grows low to the
ground, often in dry, sandy soil. It is a member of the Rose Family, a
family that also includes many fruits like apples, plums, cherries, pears,
and strawberries. The crushed leaves of most members of the family
produce an aroma of bitter almonds.

Shrubby Cinquefoil
Potentilla fruticosa

ROSE FAMILY

This low deciduous shrub is found in dry meadows, on rocky slopes, and in gravelly river courses at low to subalpine elevations. The leaves are alternate, divided into 3–7 (usually 5) leaflets that are lightly hairy, greyish-green, and often have curled edges. The flowers are golden yellow and saucer-shaped, with 5 rounded petals, usually blooming as a solitary at the end of branches. The flowers are often smaller and paler at lower elevations; larger and brighter at higher elevations.

The genus name, *Potentilla*, is explained in the note on Silverweed (*P. anserina*), shown on page 61. The species name, *fruticosa*, means "shrubby," and refers to the plant forming a low, rounded bush, usually about a metre high. The common name is from the Latin *quinque*, meaning "five," and *folium*, meaning "leaf," a reference to the fact that many *Potentilla* species have 5 leaflets and the flower parts are in fives. Shrubby Cinquefoil is a popular garden ornamental, and is easily propagated from cuttings.

Silverweed
Potentilla anserina
ROSE FAMILY

Anne Elliott image

A low, prostrate perennial that grows from thick rootstock and reddish coloured runners in moist meadows, on riverbanks, lakeshores, and slough margins. The leaves are basal, compound, toothed, and pinnate, with 7–25 leaflets per leaf. Each leaflet is silky-haired and green to silvery on top, lighter underneath. The flowers are bright yellow and solitary on leafless stems, with rounded petals in fives. The sepals are light green and hairy, and appear between the petals.

The common name is derived from the silvery colour of the leaves. The genus name, *Potentilla*, is derived from the Latin *potens*, which means "powerful," an allusion to the supposed medicinal properties of plants of this genus. The species name, *anserina*, means "goose," and has been variously explained as an allusion to the soft, hairy leaves of the plant being like down, or, alternatively, to the fact that geese might eat the plant in its native habitat. Native peoples used the roots of the plant as a food, either eating it raw or cooked. They also extracted a red dye from the plant, and used the runners as cordage material.

Narrow-Petaled Stonecrop
Sedum stenopetalum

STONECROP FAMILY

This low, erect perennial grows up to 15 cm tall in rocky and gravelly areas and grasslands. The leaves are alternate, brownish-green, and succulent, often overlapping. The star-shaped yellow flowers have 4–5 lance-shaped petals and occur in clusters at the top of the stem. Each flower has numerous yellow stamens.

The genus name, *Sedum*, is derived from the Latin *sedere*, which means "to sit," a reference to the plant's low-growing habit. The species name, *stenopetalum*, refers to the shape of the petals. The common name refers to the plant's normal habitat. Some authorities say the plant is edible, while others disagree.

Jewelweed (Touch-Me-Not)
Impatiens noli-tangere
TOUCH-ME-NOT FAMILY

Glen Lee image

This plant is an annual that grows up to 150 cm tall in moist, shady poplar woods and thickets, along stream banks, and in lake margins. The plant is succulent and leafy, with branched stems and a watery juice. The leaves are alternate, ovate, simple, irregularly toothed, and up to 12 cm long and 4 cm wide. The flowers occur mostly in pairs from the upper leaf axils. The flowers are irregularly shaped, pale yellow with red or purple flecks, and consist of a sac-like dilated sepal about 2 cm long that gradually narrows into a down-curved spur about 1 cm long.

The genus and species names are derived from the plant's explosive release of seeds when the pod-like seed capsule is touched. When this explosion occurs, seeds may be catapulted over several square metres. The genus name, *Impatiens*, is Latin meaning "impatient," and the species name, *noli-tangere*, means "touch-me-not." Some Native peoples used the plants medicinally for a variety of afflictions, including rashes, eczema, poison ivy rash, bruises, and warts. Another similar species, Spotted Touch-Me-Not (*I. capensis*) exists in similar habitat. It has bright orange to yellow flowers that are more densely spotted, and a more pouch-like spur that is bent parallel to the sac. The origin of the common name Jewelweed seems uncertain, but may be a reference to the way in which the flowers hang off the plant on thin stems.

Yellow Prairie Violet
Viola nuttallii
VIOLET FAMILY

Colin Ladyka image

This small low-growing violet occurs in open grasslands, and can be found in moist or dry habitats. The leaves are alternate, simple, narrowly lance-shaped, hairy, and tapering to the stem. The bright yellow flowers are pencilled with purple and arise from the axils of the upper leaves. The flowers have 5 petals, 5 sepals, and 5 stamens, and there is a short spur on the lowest petal. A number of flowers can occur on each plant.

This flower is a harbinger of spring, blooming early in the prairies. It is distinctive among the violets in that it has narrow, lance-shaped, hairy leaves. The species name, *nuttallii*, honours Thomas Nuttall, an English botanist and plant collector, who came to the United States early in the 1800s and collected specimens along the route followed by the Lewis and Clark expedition. Nuttall's collected specimens, unlike many of those collected by Lewis and Clark, made it back to the eastern United States for study.

Yellow Pond Lily (Yellow Water Lily)
Nuphar variegata

WATER LILY FAMILY

This plant of ponds, lakes, and slow-moving streams is perhaps the most recognizable water plant in the area. This aquatic perennial grows from a thick rootstock, producing cord-like stems. The floating leaves are borne singly on long stems, are up to 15 cm long, waxy on the surface, round and broadly oval, and heart-shaped at the base. The large flowers protrude from the water's surface, are solitary on long stalks, with 6 sepals that are showy, greenish-yellow on the outside, and tinged with red on the inside. Numerous yellow stamens surround a large pistil.

The origin of the genus name, *Nuphar*, is a matter of some dispute among the authorities. Some say it comes from the Persian word *nenuphar*; some say it comes from the Arabic word *naufar*. All agree that both words mean "pond lily." The species name, *variegata*, means "with patches of different colours," a reference to the colours in the sepals. A number of Native peoples employed the plant as a food source, eating it raw, boiled, baked, or ground into flour. Some Native peoples used the plant medicinally to treat venereal disease, make poultices, or treat horses. The plant provides cover for fish and food for waterfowl and water mammals.

Blue and Purple Flowers

This section includes flowers that are predominantly blue or purple when encountered in the field—ranging from pale blue to deep purple, light violet to lavender. Some of the lighter colours of blue and purple might shade into pinks, so if you do not find the flower you are looking for here, check the other sections of this book.

Common Butterwort
Pinguicula vulgaris

BLADDERWORT FAMILY

Glen Lee image

This small plant is one of only a few carnivorous plants in the area. It grows from fibrous roots in bogs, seeps, wetlands, stream banks, and lakeshores in valleys and the montane zone. The pale green to yellowish leaves are basal, short-stalked, somewhat overlapping, curled in at the margins, and form a rosette on the ground. The leaves have glandular hairs on their upper surface that exude a sticky substance which attracts and then ensnares small insects. The insects are then digested by the plant, enabling it to obtain nitrogen and other nutrients. The flower is pale to dark purple, solitary, and occurs atop a leafless stem.

The common name, Butterwort, is said to come from the buttery feel of the leaves, *wort* being an Old English word that means "herb" or "a plant." The genus name, *Pinguicula*, is the diminutive of the Latin word *pinguis*, which means "fat," a reference to the soft, greasy-feeling leaves of the plant.

Kalm's Lobelia
Lobelia kalmii

BLUEBELL FAMILY

Glen Lee image

This leafy-stemmed, smooth or hairy biennial or perennial often forms clumps, grows up to 30 cm tall on a slender, branching stem from fibrous roots, and occurs in bogs, ditches, damp meadows, and stream banks, preferring calcareous soil. The basal leaves are spoon-shaped or broadly oval, stalked, and usually hairy, and they appear as a rosette in the first year. The flower stalks appear in the second year, and the stem leaves are bluish-green, simple, and alternate. The few flowers are light blue and appear on slender, spreading stalks in open clusters up the stem. The corolla is 5 united petals, with white or yellow centres, and 2 lips. The upper lip has 2 small lobes, bent backwards, and the larger, lower lip has 3 lobes, which bend abruptly down at a sharp angle. The plant is closely related to cultivated Lobelias.

The genus name, *Lobelia*, honours Matthias de L'Obel, a 17th-century French physician and botanist. The species name, *kalmii*, honours Pehr Kalm, an 18th-century student of Carolus Linnaeus. Kalm discovered the species. Some Native peoples are said to have used the plant medicinally, but some members of the genus are known to cause sickness or death when so employed.

Blueweed
Echium vulgare

BORAGE FAMILY

This European import is found in roadsides, pastures, and disturbed areas throughout Canada, and is becoming a problem weed, forcing out native vegetation. The flowers are a spectacular bright blue, funnel-shaped, with unequal lobes. The flowers are distributed up a central stalk that can reach over a metre in height. The plant has an overall hairy appearance. Blueweed is also known as Viper's Bugloss and Blue Devil. At one time the plant was believed to be useful in treating snakebite. In addition, the seed shape resembles a viper's head, hence the reference to viper. Bugloss is derived from the Greek *bous*, meaning "ox," and *glossa*, meaning "tongue," the reference being that the rough leaves of this plant resemble the tongue of an ox.

The genus name, *Echium*, is derived from the Greek *echis*, meaning "viper," most probably a reference to the shape of the seed of the plant. The bristly hairs on the leaves and stem of the plant cause severe skin irritation. Infestations of this noxious weed are common in the Crowsnest area of Alberta.

Stickseed
Hackelia floribunda
BORAGE FAMILY

This plant is a hairy biennial or short-live perennial that has stiffly erect stems, and grows to a metre tall. The small, yellow-centered, blue flowers occur in loose clusters on curving stalks, near the top of the plant. The fruits are nutlets that are keeled in the middle and attached to a pyramid-shaped base. Each nutlet has rows of barbed prickles.

While the flowers on this plant are lovely to look at, the prickles on the nutlets cling easily to fur, feathers, and clothing, thus lending the plant its common name. The nutlets adhere to clothing like Velcro, and can be a huge nuisance in the late summer and autumn to anybody who walks close to the plant. The nutlets are tenacious and must be laboriously picked from socks, sweaters, and trousers. Long-haired hunting dogs can become covered in the nutlets, even to the extent that scissors are required to free the animal of the things. The nutlets are an extraordinarily effective mechanism for seed dispersal.

Tall Lungwort (Mertensia)
Mertensia paniculata

BORAGE FAMILY

This perennial grows from a woody rootstock, is usually hairy, may have multiple branches, and reaches heights of 80 cm. The plant prefers moist woods, stream banks, shaded poplar groves, and mixed forests. The basal leaves are large, prominently veined, heart-shaped, white-hairy on both sides, and long-stalked. The stem leaves are stalkless or short-stalked, rounded at the base, and tapering to the pointed tip. The blue flowers occur in drooping clusters, hanging like small, blue bells. The corolla is tubular, five-lobed, and abruptly enlarged in the middle. The flower buds often have a pinkish tinge, turning blue as they open.

The genus name, *Mertensia*, honours F. C. Mertens, an early German botanist. The common name, Lungwort, is derived from Europe, this plant's flowers being similar to the European Lungwort, a plant thought to be good in the treatment of lung diseases. Several related species occur in the area, but are uncommon. All are considerably smaller than this species, but all have the same flower conformation. Montana Bluebells is another common name that seems to be shared by all of the Mertensias.

Blue Clematis
Clematis occidentalis

BUTTERCUP FAMILY

A plant of shaded riverine woods and thickets, the Clematis is a climbing, slightly hairy, reddish-stemmed vine that attaches itself to other plants by slender tendrils. The flowers have 4–5 sepals and are purplish to blue in colour, with dark veins. The flowers resemble crepe paper.

The genus and common name is derived from the Greek word *klema*, meaning "vine branch or tendril." The Blackfoot called the plant "ghost's lariat," a reference to the fact that the vine would entangle their feet when they walked through it. Many tribes used the plant to weave mats and bags. The whole plant is toxic if ingested. Clematis also occurs in yellow (*C. tangutica*) and white (*C. ligusticifolia*), and often goes by the locally common name of Virgin's Bower.

Blue Columbine
Aquilegia brevistyla
BUTTERCUP FAMILY

This plant occurs in deciduous, coniferous, and mixed woods, meadows, and riverine environments, and grows to heights of 80 cm. It has slender, slightly purplish hairy stems. The attractive flower can be nodding or ascending, with yellowish or white petals, and 5 blue to purplish reflexed sepals. The bluish-green leaflets with scalloped tips appear in threes. Columbines have a very distinctive floral structure, and are usually unmistakable.

The name Columbine is derived from the Latin *columbina*, meaning "dove like," it being said that the petals resemble a group of doves drinking at a dish. The origin of the genus name, *Aquilegia*, is fraught with some uncertainty. One school of thought attributes the name to the Latin *aquila*, meaning "eagle," a reference to the long, claw-like spur on the flower, supposedly resembling an eagle's talon. The other school of thought is that the name is derived from *aqua*, meaning "water," and *legere*, meaning "to collect," as little drops of nectar collect at the ends of the spurs. An interesting juxtaposition, with the war symbol eagle on one side, and the peace symbol dove on the other. Bumblebees and butterflies are drawn to the Columbines to collect the nectar. Columbines also appear in western North America in yellow (*A. flavescens*) and red (*A. formosa*).

Low Larkspur
Delphinium bicolor

BUTTERCUP FAMILY

A plant of open woods, grasslands, and slopes, Larkspurs are easily recognized for their showy, highly modified flowers. The irregular petals are whitish to bluish, with sepals that are blue to violet. The upper sepal forms a large, hollow, nectar-producing spur. The flowers bloom up the stem in a loose, elongated cluster.

The genus name, *Delphinium*, is derived from the Greek word *delphin*, which means "dolphin," a reference to the plant's nectaries, which are said to resemble old pictures of dolphins. The common name is said to have originated because the spur on the flower resembles the spur on the foot of a lark. The flowers are favoured by bumblebees and butterflies. The plant contains delphinine, a toxic alkaloid, and is poisonous to cattle and humans. Tall Larkspur (*D. glaucum*) also occurs in the area. It has similar flowers to this species, but Tall Larkspur grows to heights of up to 2 m and has numerous flowers.

Prairie Crocus
Pulsatilla patens
BUTTERCUP FAMILY

This plant is widespread and common in grasslands, dry meadows, and mountain slopes. It is usually one of the first wildflowers to bloom in the spring, and can occur in huge numbers. The flowers are usually solitary, various blues to purples in colour, and cup-shaped. White varieties are sometimes seen. It is interesting to note that the flower blooms before the basal leaves appear. The plant has many basal leaves, palmately divided into 3 main leaflets, and again divided into narrow linear segments. The leaves on the flower stem appear in a whorl of 3. The fruits are large spherical clusters of silky-haired, long-plumed seeds that are distributed by the wind.

The Prairie Crocus is also known as a Pasque Flower, pasque being an old French word for Easter, and referencing the blooming of this flower around the time of Easter. The texture of the petals is as soft as down. Prairie Crocus is the floral emblem of the Province of Manitoba. Prairie Crocus contains a substance called protoanemonin, an irritant that can produce rashes

Blue Lettuce
Lactuca tatarica ssp. *pulchella*

COMPOSITE FAMILY

A plant of fields, roadsides, meadows, shores, and stream banks, often found on moist, heavy soil. The flowers have pale to dark blue ray florets, toothed at the tip. There are no disk florets. The leaves are hairless, lobed below, and simple above.

The genus name, *Lactuca*, is derived from the Latin *lac*, meaning "milk," and refers to the milky sap from the plant. Plants of this genus are particularly enjoyed by horses, apparently, and they are sometimes referred to as Horseweeds.

Bull Thistle
Cirsium vulgare
COMPOSITE FAMILY

A Eurasian weed introduced to North America that is common in pastures, waste places, clearings, and roadsides. The flowers are large, composite heads with purple disk flowers and no ray flowers. The flower heads are bulbous and covered in sharp spikes. The flower structure is extraordinarily intricate when examined closely. The leaves, both basal and stem, are lance-shaped, deeply lobed, and spiny, clasping the stem. The Bull Thistle will grow to heights of over 2 m, and will produce a multitude of flowers.

All thistles have spines on their leaf edges, but the Bull Thistle is the only one with a spiny leaf surface. The flowers are a favourite of bees and butterflies. The thistle generally is the national emblem of Scotland, legend having it that a soldier in an invading Danish army stepped on a thistle and cried out in pain, awaking and alerting the Scottish encampment, who rose and repelled the invading army. The thistle was thereafter considered to be the guardian of Scotland. Bull Thistle is also known locally as Spear Thistle.

Canada Thistle
Cirsium arvense
COMPOSITE FAMILY

Despite the common name, this noxious weed was introduced to North America from Eurasia. The plant grows to over a metre in height from a thin, white, creeping rhizome. The flowers occur in heads at the tops of the multiple branches. The flowers are usually pinkish to mauve, but they may be white. The leaves are alternate and oblong to lance-shaped, with wavy margins.

The species name of this plant, *arvense*, means "of cultivated fields," and the plant certainly lives up to its name. By combining a creeping rhizome and tremendous seed distribution, the plant will quickly take over areas where it grows. If the rhizome is cut or broken by farming machinery, the spread of the plant is exacerbated. Canada Thistle is dioecious—that is, male and female flowers occur on separate plants.

Common Burdock
Arctium minus

COMPOSITE FAMILY

A plant of pastures, roadsides, fencerows, and disturbed sites, Common Burdock is erect with spreading branches, and grows to over a metre in height. The flowers appear at the ends of the branches as purplish to pinkish tubular protrusions with disk florets only. The outer bracts are decidedly hooked at the ends, and form a ball around the inflorescence, making the plant appear to be furry and unkempt.

Arctium species are native to and widespread in Eurasia. In Japan the edible roots of the plants are known as *gobo*. It is said that the hooks on the involucral bracts of this plant inspired the creation of Velcro. These hooks are extraordinarily efficient in disseminating the seeds of the plant, clinging as they do to fur on animals and clothing on humans who encounter the plant in the field.

Parry's Townsendia
Townsendia parryi
COMPOSITE FAMILY

This tap-rooted reddish-stemmed perennial blooms in the early spring, and appears on dry hills, stream banks, gravelly slopes, and grassy areas from prairie to alpine elevations. Most of the leaves are basal and form a rosette at ground level. The stems, leaves, and bracts are covered in white hairs. The relatively large flowers appear low to the ground on short stems, and they consist of broad ray flowers of violet to purple, surrounding bright yellow disk flowers.

The genus name, *Townsendia*, honours David Townsend, a 19th-century American botanist. The species name, *parryi*, honours Charles C. Parry, a 19th-century English naturalist and botanical explorer who came to America and catalogued a large number of plants. The Blackfoot boiled the roots of some Townsendias to make a concoction for treating ailments in horses. Another Townsendia occurs in the area, Low Townsendia (*T. hookeri),* but its ray flowers are white to pink and almost stemless. Low Townsendia is a fairly rare plant.

Showy Aster
Aster conspicuus
COMPOSITE FAMILY

This plant is widespread and common in low to mid-elevations in moist to dry open forests, openings, clearings, and meadows. The flowers are few to many composite heads on glandular stalks, with 15–35 violet ray flowers, and yellow disk flowers. The stem leaves are egg-shaped to elliptical, with sharp toothed edges and clasping bases.

Aster is the Latin name for "star," referring to the flower's shape. *Conspicuus* means "conspicuous," a reference to the showy flowers. Some Native peoples soaked the roots of the plant in water and used the liquid to treat boils. The leaves were also used as a poultice for that purpose.

Smooth Blue Aster
Aster laevis

COMPOSITE FAMILY

This plant inhabits open wooded areas, meadows, coulees, and ditches, often on gravelly soil. The plants are erect, up to 120 cm tall, and can form large colonies. The flowers are composed of pale to dark purple or bluish ray florets, surrounding bright yellow disk florets.

The genus name, *Aster*, is derived from the Latin for "star," a reference to the general shape of the flower. Smooth Blue Aster is believed to be a selenium absorber, and therefore dangerous to livestock who consume it. Selenium is a chemical element that is cumulative in the digestive system, and too much can lead to symptoms like the blind staggers.

Smooth Fleabane
Erigeron glabellus
COMPOSITE FAMILY

Anne Elliott image

This erect perennial or biennial has hairy simple or branched stems, and reaches heights of 60 cm in meadows, along roadsides, in moist grasslands, and in open woods, from the prairie to subalpine elevations. The leaves are mainly basal, somewhat hairy, and dark green. The lower leaves are lance-shaped and up to 10 cm long, with the stem leaves gradually reducing up the stem. The flower heads may number up to 5 per stem, and are typical of the Composite Family, with over 100 blue or lilac (sometimes white), thin ray florets, surrounding bright yellow disk florets. The bracts are narrow and hairy, with a brown midvein.

The origin of the common name and genus name is explained in the note on Tufted Fleabane (*E. caespitosus*), shown on page 134. The species name, *glabellus*, is Latin meaning "smooth," but the reference is confusing because this plant is most often hairy, not smooth. The plant is sometimes referred to as Smooth Daisy. Philadelphia Fleabane (*E. philadelphicus*) is a very similar species that occurs in the same habitat, but it has leaves that are spoon-shaped and more clasping at the base.

Lilac-Flowered Beardtongue
Penstemon gracilis

FIGWORT FAMILY

Glen Lee image

This plant is one of a number of Beardtongues that occur in the area. It inhabits moist grasslands and slough margins, and grows to heights of 45 cm. The leaves are opposite, greyish-green, smooth, lance-shaped, and slightly toothed. The flowers are lilac in colour and typical of the Beardtongues, having a tubular corolla of 5 petals and 2 lips, with the lower lip having 3 lobes with soft hairs inside, and the upper lip having 2 lobes. The flowers in this species are about 2 cm long, and are borne on the stem in interrupted rings along the spike.

The genus name, *Penstemon*, is derived from the Greek *pente*, meaning "five," and *stemon*, meaning "stamen," a reference to the 5 stamens of plants of this genus. The common name, Beardtongue, arises from the hairy, tongue-like staminode in the throat of the flowers in this genus. A number of Penstemons are found in the area.

Small Flowered Beardtongue
Penstemon procerus

FIGWORT FAMILY

This plant grows to heights of 40 cm, and appears from low to alpine elevations, usually in dry to moist open forests, grassy clearings, meadows, and disturbed areas. Most of the blunt to lance- shaped leaves appear in opposite pairs up the stem. The flowers are small, funnel-shaped, blue to purple, and appear in one to several tight clusters arranged in whorls around the stem and at its tip.

The genus name, *Penstemon*, is derived from the Greek *penta*, meaning "five" and *stemon*, meaning "thread," a reference to the 5 thread-like stamens common to the family. The genus is a large and complex group of plants. There are dozens of Penstemons in the Rocky Mountains and many will hybridize freely, adding even more confusion to the specific identification. Small-Flowered Beardtongue can usually be identified by its small, tightly packed flowers that appear in whorls around the stem. Another common Penstemon in the same habitat is Yellow Penstemon (*P. confertus*), which has a similar flower construction with yellow flowers. Two other common names applied to Small-Flowered Beardtongue are Slender Beardtongue and Small Flowered Penstemon. The common name, Beardtongue, is applied to the Penstemons because the flowers have hairs in the throat of the flower, thus a "bearded tongue."

Smooth Blue Beardtongue
Penstemon nitidus

FIGWORT FAMILY

This erect, often branched perennial usually has several stems that grow to 30 cm tall, and it often occurs in clumps on dry grassy slopes, eroded areas, and sandy soils. The stems are hairless. The oval to lance-shaped leaves are opposite, thick and fleshy, pale green, and covered with a greyish bloom, similar to the skin on a grape. The blue flowers are numerous and occur in dense clusters from the leaf axils at the top of the plant. The flowers are tube-shaped and up to 2 cm long, and have purple pencilling inside the lower floral lip. There are 2 lips, the lower being three-lobed with soft, smooth hairs, and the upper being two-lobed.

The origin of the common name, Beardtongue, and the genus name, *Penstemon*, is explained in the narrative on Lilac-Flowered Beardtongue (*P. gracilis*), shown on page 84. This Beardtongue is an early bloomer on the prairie, and its bright blue flowers on a smooth stem are quite striking. A number of Beardtongues of various colours occur in the area.

Blue Flax
Linum perenne ssp. *lewisii*
FLAX FAMILY

A plant of dry, exposed hillsides, grasslands, roadsides, and gravelly river flats. The five-petaled flowers are pale purplish-blue, with darkish guidelines, yellowish at the base. The leaves are alternate, simple, and stalkless. The flowers appear on very slender stems that are constantly moving, even with the smallest of breezes.

The genus name, *Linum*, is derived from the Greek *linon*, meaning "thread." Each bud of this delicate flower blooms for only one day. The plant has been cultivated for various uses, notably oil and linen, since ancient times.

Hairy Four-O'Clock (Umbrellawort)
Mirabilis hirsuta
FOUR-O'CLOCK FAMILY

This perennial grows from a heavy, woody taproot in native pastures in the area, and reaches 60 cm in height. The plant is covered in short hairs. The leaves are opposite, variable in shape, and up to 10 cm long. The flowers are bluish to pinkish, and often occur in groups of 3 on the upper one-half of the plant.

The common name Four-O'Clock comes from the fact that many members of the genus have flowers that open in the late afternoon. The genus name, *Mirabilis*, is derived from Latin, and means "wonderful." The species name, *hirsuta*, is derived from Latin, and means "hairy." Plants in the genus are often referred to as Umbrellaworts. The plant was first described for science by Frederick Pursh.

Northern Gentian
Gentianella amarella (also *Gentiana amerella*)
GENTIAN FAMILY

A plant of moist places in meadows, moist woods, ditches, and stream banks, these lovely flowers are first sighted by their star-like formation winking at the top of the corolla tube amidst adjacent grasses. The plant is most often small, standing only 15–20 cm, though taller specimens are sometimes seen. The flowers appear in clusters in the axils of the upper stem leaves, the leaves being opposite, and appearing almost to be small hands holding up the flowers for inspection.

The genus name, *Gentianella*, comes from Gentius, a king of ancient Illyria, a coastal region on the Adriatic Sea. Gentius was said to have discovered medicinal properties in the plants of this genus. The species name, *amarella*, is derived from the Latin *amarus*, meaning "bitter," a reference to the bitter alkaloids contained in the plant's juices. The plant is also commonly referred to as Felwort. That name is derived from Old English *feld*, which means "field," and *wort*, which means "herb" or "a plant." A similar plant called the Small Fringed Gentian (*G. procera*), occurs in the northern and eastern parts of the area. Its flowers are deep sky blue, and its corolla is four-parted.

Oblong-Leaved Gentian (Prairie Gentian)
Gentiana affinis

GENTIAN FAMILY

Glen Lee image

This tufted, smooth, leafy perennial often forms colonies, grows up to 30 cm tall (though usually smaller), and grows from thick, fleshy roots. It occurs in moist slough margins, moist meadows and prairies, and along riverbanks. The plant is sometimes erect, but is often decumbent—reclining on the ground with tip ascending. The leaves are opposite, simple, up to 4 cm long, and, as suggested by the name, oblong or lance-shaped, with somewhat pointed ends. The dark blue to purplish flowers occur singly or severally at the top of the stem. The corolla is up to 3 cm long, funnel-shaped, five-lobed, and is often marked with green.

The origin of the genus name, *Gentiana* is explained in the narrative on Northern Gentian (*Gentianella amarella*), shown on page 89. Plants of this genus are also commonly referred to as Felworts. That name is derived from Old English *feld*, which means "field," and *wort*, which means "herb" or "a plant."

Sticky Purple Geranium
Geranium viscosissimum

GERANIUM FAMILY

A plant of moist grasslands, open woods, and thickets. The plants can grow up to 60 cm tall. The flowers have large, showy, rose-purple to bluish petals that are strongly veined with purple. The long-stalked leaves are deeply lobed and split into 5–7 sharply toothed divisions, appearing in opposite pairs along the stem. There are sticky, glandular hairs covering the stems, leaves, and some flower parts. The fruit is an elongated, glandular hairy capsule, with a long beak shaped like a stork's or crane's bill.

The genus name, *Geranium*, is derived from the Greek *geranos*, meaning "crane," a reference to the fruit being shaped like a crane's bill. Indeed, Crane's Bill is an oft-used common name for the Geraniums. The species name, *viscosissimum*, is the Latin superlative for *viscid*, which means "thick and gluey." The sticky, glandular hairs appearing on the stems and leaves effectively protect the plant from pollen theft by ants and other crawling insects. The Sticky Purple Geranium is very similar to a European import that has naturalized in dry grasslands in western North America, the Stork's Bill (*Erodium cicutarium*). Interestingly enough, *Erodium* is Greek for "heron," another bird with a long, pointed bill. The ornithological references to storks, herons, and cranes can certainly lend some confusion when common names are applied to wildflowers of the Geranium Family.

Harebell
Campanula rotundifolia

HAREBELL FAMILY

This plant is widespread in a variety of habitats, including grasslands, gullies, moist forests, openings, clearings, and rocky open ground. The flowers are purplish, blue, rarely white, bell-shaped, with hairless sepals nodding on a thin stem in loose clusters. The leaves are thin on the stem and lance-shaped. The basal leaves are heart-shaped and coarsely toothed, but they usually wither before the flowers appear.

The genus name, *Campanula*, is derived from the Latin *campana*, meaning "bell." *Campanula* is the diminutive of *campana*, thus "little bell." The species name, *rotundifolia*, refers to the round basal leaves. This is the Bluebell of Scotland, and one school of thought holds that Harebell comes from a contraction of "heatherbell." Another school of thought holds that Harebell is a misspelling of "hairbell," the reference being to the hair-thin stems on which the flowers appear. Where Harebells occur, they can be in profusion and can cast a purple hue to the area when they are in bloom. The Cree were said to have chopped and dried the roots to make into compresses for stopping bleeding and to reduce swelling. The foliage contains alkaloids and is avoided by browsing animals.

Western Bog-Laurel (Swamp Laurel)
Kalmia microphylla

HEATH FAMILY

This low-growing evergreen shrub occurs in cool bogs, on stream banks, and lakeshores from low to subalpine elevations. The leaves are leathery, dark green above and greyish white beneath, often with the margins rolled under. The flowers are pink to rose-coloured, with the petals fused together to form a saucer or bowl, appearing on a reddish stalk. There are 10 purple-tipped stamens protruding from the petals.

The genus name, *Kalmia*, is to honour Peter Kalm, a student of Carolus Linnaeus at Uppsala University in Sweden. Linnaeus was a prominent botanist who developed binomial nomenclature for plants. The leaves and flowers of this plant contain poisonous alkaloids that can be fatal to humans and livestock if ingested.

Blue-Eyed Grass
Sisyrinchium montanum

IRIS FAMILY

These beautiful flowers are in the Iris Family, and can be found scattered among the grasses of moist meadows from the prairies to the subalpine zones. The distinctively flattened stems grow to heights of up to 30 cm, and are twice as tall as the grass-like basal leaves. The blue flower is star-shaped, with 3 virtually identical petals and sepals, each tipped with a minute point. There is a bright yellow eye in the centre of the flower. The blossoms are very short-lived, wilting usually within one day, to be replaced by fresh ones on the succeeding day.

The genus name, *Sisyrinchium*, was a name applied by Theophrastus, a disciple of Aristotle who refined the philosopher's work in botany and natural sciences in ancient Greece. It is a reference to a plant allied to the Iris. The species name, *montanum*, means "of the mountains," though, indeed, the plant is also found in other environments. The flower has a number of locally common names, including Montana Blue-Eyed Grass, Idaho Blue-Eyed Grass, Eyebright, Grass Widow, and Blue Star.

Giant Hyssop
Agastache foeniculum
MINT FAMILY

A plant common in thickets and along streams, this member of the Mint Family is erect and grows to heights of up to 100 cm. The stem is square in cross-section, typical of the Mint Family. The leaves are opposite, oval in shape, coarsely toothed, with pointed tips. The blue to purple flowers are densely packed and appear in interrupted clusters along the top of the stem.

The genus name, *Agastache*, is derived from the Greek *agan*, meaning "much," and *stachys*, meaning "spike," a reference to the way the flowers appear on the top of the stem. The species name, *foeniculum*, means "scent like fennel." Native peoples used the leaves of the plant for making a tea and as a flavouring in foods. The flowers were often collected for medicine bundles.

Heal-All (Self-Heal)
Prunella vulgaris
MINT FAMILY

This is a plant found in moist woods, along stream banks and lakeshores, and in fields from the prairie to the montane zone. The flowers occur in terminal clusters, usually surrounded by the upper leaves. The bracts are kidney-shaped to oval, with spines at the tips and hairs along the margins. The few leaves are opposite, smooth, and sparsely hairy. The plant is small and sprawling, and square-stemmed.

The genus name, *Prunella,* is most likely derived from the German *braune,* meaning "quinsy" or "angina," a condition this plant was used to cure. The traditional use of the plant for healing internal and external bleeding gives rise to the common name, but tests on the plant's extracts have not revealed any biochemical basis for the claims of healing. Parts of this small flower have been used by Native peoples to relieve boils, cuts, bruises, internal bleeding, and swellings. The Cree treated sore throats with an extract from the plant. The Blackfoot used it as an eyewash, and treated horses' saddle sores with it. The leaves can be brewed into a tea.

Marsh Hedge-Nettle
Stachys palustris
MINT FAMILY

A plant of wetland margins, stream banks, marshes, and wet ditches, Marsh Hedge-Nettle grows erect to heights of up to 40 cm. The stems are square, and the leaves are opposite and simple, lance-shaped, and hairy. The flowers are pale purple and appear at the top of the spike, often in interrupted fashion.

The genus name, *Stachys*, is Greek for "spike," referring to the inflorescence type. The species name, *palustris*, is Latin meaning "of wet places."

Marsh Skullcap
Scutellaria galericulata
MINT FAMILY

This member of the Mint Family grows to heights of 80 cm at low to mid elevations in wetlands, along lakeshores, on stream banks, and in ditches. The leaves are opposite, oval to lance-shaped, and are irregularly scalloped along the blades. The stem is square, typical of the Mint Family. The trumpet-shaped flowers have a hooded upper lip and a broad hairless lower lip, and are blue to purplish-pink, marked with white. The flowers occur as solitary on slender stalks, or as pairs in the leaf axils.

The common name for the plant comes from the hood-like appearance of the upper lip of the flower. The species name, *galericulata* means "helmet shaped." The plant contains a flavonoid called scutellaria that has sedative and anti-spasmodic properties. A tea made from the plant has long been used by herbalists to treat nervous disorders.

Wild Mint (Canada Mint)
Mentha arvensis (also *Mentha canadensis)*
MINT FAMILY

This plant inhabits wetland marshes, moist woods, banks and shores of streams and lakes, and sometimes lives in shallow water. The purplish, to pinkish, to bluish flowers are crowded in dense clusters in the upper leaf axils. The leaves are opposite, prominently veined, and highly scented of mint if crushed. The stems are square in cross section and hairy.

The genus name, *Mentha*, is from the Greek *Minthe*, a mythological nymph loved by Pluto. A jealous Proserpine changed the nymph into a mint plant. The species name, *arvensis*, means "growing in fields." The strong, distinctive taste of mint plants is from their volatile oils. The leaves have long been used fresh, dried, and frozen as a flavouring and for teas. Some Native peoples used the leaves to flavour meat and pemmican, and lined dried meat containers with mint leaves prior to winter storage. Strong mint teas were used by Native peoples and European settlers as a treatment for coughs, colds, and fevers.

Dame's Rocket (Dame's Violet)
Hesperis matronalis

MUSTARD FAMILY

This member of the Mustard Family was introduced from Eurasia into North America during colonial days as an ornamental plant, and it has spread extensively, now being found throughout Canada and much of the United States. In many areas it is looked upon as an invasive, noxious weed, though it is still available and sold as an ornamental by some nurseries. Typically it inhabits disturbed sites, waste ground, thickets, woods, and road and railsides. The plant is erect and grows to heights of over a metre. The leaves are alternate, lance-shaped, predominately clasping on the stem, hairy on both sides, and become progressively smaller up the stem. The flowers occur in showy clusters at the top of the stem. Each flower is four-petaled, purple to blue to white in colour, and fragrant.

The genus name, *Hesperis*, is derived from the Greek *hesperos*, which means "evening," the reference being that the flowers are said to have an enhanced aroma near evening. The species name, *matronalis*, is said to derive from the flower being a favourite of Roman matrons, ergo the reference to Dame in the common name. Dame's Rocket goes by a number of other common names, including Dame's Violet, Dame's Wort, Sweet Rocket, and Mother Of The Evening.

Spotted Coralroot
Corallorhiza maculata

ORCHID FAMILY

A plant of moist woods and bogs, this orchid grows from extensive coral-like rhizomes. The purple to brownish flowers have purple or red spots on the white lip. A number of flowers appear on each stem, loosely arranged up the stem. The leaves are reduced to sheaths that surround and somewhat conceal the base of the purplish stem.

The genus name, *Corallorhiza*, is derived from the Greek *korallion*, meaning "coral," and *rhiza*, meaning "root," a reference to the rhizomes from which the plant grows. Two other Coralroots occur in the same habitat as the Spotted—the Pale Coralroot (*C. trifida*) and the Striped Coralroot (*C. striata*). The Coralroots are saprophytes, i.e., a plant that absorbs its nutrition from decaying organic matter and lacks any green pigment (chlorophyll) used by most plants for food production.

Striped Coralroot
Corallorhiza striata

ORCHID FAMILY

A plant of moist woods and bogs, this orchid grows from extensive coral-like rhizomes. The pink to yellowish-pink flowers have purplish stripes on the sepals, and the lowest petal forms a tongue-shaped lip. A number of flowers appear on each stem, loosely arranged up the stem. The leaves are reduced to sheaths that surround, and somewhat conceal, the base of the purplish stem.

The genus name, *Corallorhiza*, is derived from the Greek *korallion*, meaning "coral," and *rhiza*, meaning "root," a reference to the rhizomes from which the plant grows. Two other Coralroots occur in the same habitat as the Striped—the Pale Coralroot (*C. trifida*) and the Spotted Coralroot (*C. maculata*). Of the three, the Striped Coralroots have the largest flowers. The Coralroots are saprophytes, i.e., a plant that absorbs its nutrition from decaying organic matter and lacks any green pigment (chlorophyll) used by most plants for food production.

Venus Slipper
Calypso bulbosa
ORCHID FAMILY

An orchid found in shaded, moist, coniferous forests. The flowers are solitary and nodding on leafless stems. The flower has pinkish to purplish sepals and mauve side petals. The lip is whitish or purplish with red to purple spots or stripes, and is hairy yellow inside. The flower is on the top of a single stalk, with a deeply wrinkled appearance. A small but extraordinarily beautiful flower that blooms in the early spring, often occurring in colonies.

The Venus Slipper has many common names, including Fairy Slipper and Calypso Orchid. The genus name, *Calypso*, is derived from Greek mythology, Calypso being the daughter of Atlas. *Calypso* means "concealment," and is very apt, given that this flower is very easy to miss, being small, delicate, and growing in out-of-the-way places. The species name, *bulbosa*, refers to the bulb-like corm from which the flower grows. Do not attempt to transplant this flower. It needs specific fungi in the soil to grow successfully. Its range has diminished over time, owing to over-picking.

Ascending Purple Milk-Vetch
Astragalus adsurgens

PEA FAMILY

This tufted, erect or spreading perennial grows up to 50 cm tall from a heavy taproot in grasslands and meadows. The leaves are pinnately compound, greyish-green in colour, and hairy. Leaflets number 9–25. The plant usually has 12 or more stems and forms clumps up to 60 cm wide. The flowers occur in dense rounded or cylindrical clusters, and may be white, purplish, or lavender in colour. The standard usually has dark markings, and the keel is dark-tinged.

The origin of the genus name, *Astragalus*, is explained in the note on Two-Grooved Milk-Vetch (*A. bisulcatus*), shown on page 110. The species name, *adsurgens*, is derived from Latin and means "rising up near," most probably a reference to the erect stems of the plant. The plant is also known as Standing Milk-Vetch and Lavender Milk-Vetch. It was first described for science by 18th-century German botanist Peter Pallas.

Indian Breadroot
Psoralea esculenta

PEA FAMILY

Anne Elliott image

This short-stemmed, white-hairy perennial grows from an enlarged tuberous root to heights of 30 cm, and occurs on high, dry prairie grasslands and slopes. The leaves are blue-green and palmately compound, with 3–5 broadly lance-shaped leaflets which are smooth above, and hairy underneath. The shape of the leaves is very reminiscent of Lupines, and the plant has been referred to as a "stunted Lupine." The flowers are numerous, light bluish-purple in colour, and occur in dense clusters.

The genus name, *Psoralea*, is derived from the Greek *psora*, which means "itch or mange," a reference to the rough, scaly glands on some members of the genus. The skin disease psoriasis has the same derivation. The roots of the plant are rich in starch and sugar, and they were prepared in various ways and eaten by Native peoples and early settlers. The roots were also ground into a flour for baking. Silverleaf Psoralea (*P. argophylla*), another member of the genus, occurs in similar habitat, but it is rarer than this species, has darker blue flowers, and is extremely hairy in appearance.

Purple Milk-Vetch
Astragalus agrestis
PEA FFAMILY

This plant occurs from the prairie to subalpine elevations, growing in grasslands and meadows. It is a low-growing, hairy plant that may be erect or decumbent. The leaves are compound, with 9–23 spear-shaped leaflets that are often notched on the blunt ends. The flowers are purple to pink, and occur in densely packed, rounded clusters which are enclosed by a calyx that has greyish to blackish hairs.

The origin of the genus name, *Astragalus*, is explained in the note on Two-Grooved Milk-Vetch (*A. bisulcatus*), shown on page 110. The species name, *agrestis*, is derived from Latin and means "pertaining to fields or cultivated lands."

Purple Prairie-Clover
Petalostemon purpureum

PEA FAMILY

Anne Elliott image

This perennial is a many-stemmed, decumbent or erect, smooth, leafy plant that grows up to 60 cm tall from a thick rootstock. It occurs on hillsides, in open prairie, at roadsides, and on eroded slopes in badlands. The leaves are medium-green, alternate, and pinnately compound, with 7–10 narrow, linear leaflets. The leaflets are usually blunt-tipped and often notched. The small flowers are numerous, dark-purple to rose in colour, and each has 5 petals of almost the same size and shape, without the keel typical of pea flowers. The flowers occur in a densely packed terminal head or spike at the top of the stem. The flowers are most often seen at the base of the spike, with a bare area above, similar to coneflowers.

The genus name, *Petalostemon*, is derived from the Greek *petalon*, meaning "petal," and *stemon*, meaning "stamen," a reference to the petal-like stamens of some members of the genus. Another, similar flower occurs in the same habitat—White Prairie-Clover (*P. candidum*)—but it has white flowers.

Showy Locoweed
Oxytropis splendens

PEA FAMILY

This attractive member of the Pea Family has silvery leaves growing from a branched, woody rootstock. The flower stalk is elongated, and holds dense clusters of numerous flowers above the silvery leaves. The flowers are purple to bluish, and shaped like other members of the Pea Family.

Locoweeds are poisonous to cattle, horses, and sheep because the plants contain an alkaloid that can cause blind staggering, thus the common name. There is now some evidence that the plants in this genus (together with some others) may be storers of selenium, a toxic element that could give rise to the blind staggers in animals that ingest the plants. The genus name, *Oxytropis*, comes from the Greek *oxys*, meaning "sharp," and *tropis*, meaning "keel," a reference to the flower shape.

Silky Lupine
Lupinus sericeus

PEA FAMILY

A leafy, erect, tufted perennial with stout stems that appears in sandy to gravelly grasslands, open woods, and roadsides, often growing in dense clumps or bunches. The plant can reach heights of up to 80 cm. The flowers are showy, in dense, long, terminal clusters, and display a variety of colours in blues and purples, occasionally white and yellow. Tremendous colour variation can occur, even in plants that are very close to each other. Flowers have a typical pea shape, with a strongly truncated keel and a pointed tip. The leaves of Lupines are very distinctive. They are palmately compound and alternate on the stem, with 5–9 very narrow leaflets that have silky hairs on both sides.

The genus name, *Lupinus*, is derived from the Latin *lupus*, meaning "wolf." That much appears to be accepted, but how this name came to be applied to this plant is open to contention. Perhaps the best explanation is that the plants were once thought (inaccurately) to be a devourer or robber of soil nutrients, hence a wolf. In fact, the root nodules of Lupines produce a nitrogen-fixing bacteria that actually tends to enrich poor soil. The species name, *sericeus*, is from the Latin *sericus*, meaning "silk," a reference to the soft, silky hairs that cover the plant. The fruits of Lupine contain an alkaloid and may be poisonous to some livestock, particularly sheep.

Two-Grooved Milk-Vetch
Astragalus bisulcatus

PEA FAMILY

Anne Elliott image

This plant grows, often in large clumps, on dry hillsides and in coulees in the southern prairies. The clumps may cover an area up to a metre in diameter, with a number of flowering stems arising to 60 cm tall, from a single taproot. The leaves are greyish-green, opposite, and pinnately compound, with 17–27 elliptic leaflets. The flowers are deep purple in colour, and occur in dense clusters of 20 or more flowers at the ends of the stalks. Both the flowers and the resulting pods point downwards. The pods are clearly marked by 2 deep grooves on the upper side, giving the plant its common name.

The origin of the genus name appears to be in some doubt. Some authorities say it is a reference to an Old World plant, the specifics of which have been lost. Others say it is derived from a Greek word which means "ankle bone," and is a reference to the pod shape of some members of the genus. The members of the genus appear to be concentrators of selenium, a chemical element related to sulphur, which can be toxic to livestock who feed on the plants. Narrow-Leaved Milk-Vetch (*A. pectinatus*), is another Milk-Vetch that occurs in similar habitat. It is smaller than this species, has fewer leaflets, and has cream-coloured flowers. Plants of this genus might be confused with those of *Oxytropis*, the Locoweeds. See Cushion Milk-Vetch (*A. triphyllus*), shown on page 53.

Shooting Star
Dodecatheon pulchellum

PRIMROSE FAMILY

This beautiful plant is scattered and locally common at low to alpine elevations in warm, dry climates, grasslands, mountain meadows, and stream banks. The leaves appear in a basal rosette, lance- to spatula-shaped. The flowers appear, one to several, nodding atop a leafless stalk. The flowers are purple to lavender, occasionally white, with corolla lobes turned backwards. The stamens are united into a yellow to orange tube, from which the style and anthers protrude.

A harbinger of spring, these lovely flowers bloom in huge numbers, and the grasslands take on a purple hue when the Shooting Stars are in bloom. The genus name, *Dodecatheon*, is derived from the Greek *dodeka*, meaning "twelve," and *theos*, meaning "gods," thus a plant that is protected by twelve gods. The species name, *pulchellum*, is Latin for "beautiful." Native peoples used an infusion from this plant as an eyewash, and some looked upon the plant as a charm to obtain wealth. Some tribes mashed the flowers to make a pink dye for their arrows. The common name is an apt description of the flower, with the turned back petals streaming behind the stamens.

Purple Avens
Geum rivale
ROSE FAMILY

Anne Elliott image

This is a plant of marshes, wet meadows, and swampy ground.
The basal leaves are long-stemmed, lyre-shaped, coarsely toothed, and appear in threes. The stem leaves are smaller, somewhat hairy, and appear in threes, with the terminal segment being three-lobed. The flowers are brownish-yellow to purple, hairy, and appear solitary and nodding at the top of the branched stem. The fruits are achenes in a feathery head.

The genus name, *Geum*, is said to be derived from the Greek *geyo*, which means "to impart a relish," a reference to the use of a similar Mediterranean species. *Geum* species are highly astringent and are favoured by herbalists for treating a variety of ailments. Native tribes likewise used them for treating coughs, toothache, and diarrhea. A similar species, Old Man's Whiskers or Three-Flowered Avens (*G. triflorum*) exists in the area, but the flowers are different, and it prefers less moist environments.

Bog Violet
Viola nephrophylla
VIOLET FAMILY

A beautiful small violet that grows in moist meadows, stream banks, and woods. The leaves and flower stalks arise from the base of the plant. The leaves are oval to kidney-shaped, smooth, and scalloped on the margins. The purple to blue flowers each have a spur 2–3 mm long.

Violets are high in vitamins C and A, and have been used as food since early Greek and Roman times. They are still cultivated for that purpose in some parts of Europe. The young leaves and flower buds may be used in salads or boiled.

Crowfoot Violet (Prairie Violet)
Viola pedatifida

VIOLET FAMILY

Colin Ladyka image

This perennial occurs on open dry prairies and hillsides mostly in the eastern part of the prairies, and arises from a short, vertical rootstock to heights of up to 20 cm. The leaves are all basal and erect, stemless, cleft into 3 lobes, which are then cleft again into 3 or 4 lobes. The flowers are relatively large for the size of the plant. The flowers are violet blue and typical of flowers of the Violet Family. The 3 lower petals are whitish at the inside base, and are heavily bearded inside the flower.

The species name, *pedatifida*, is derived from Latin and means "pedately cleft," a reference to the leaves being divided from a central point, with divisions also deeply cleft. The shape of the leaves gives rise to the common name, it being said that the clefts in the leaves are reminiscent of the foot of a bird. Violets are used worldwide as a food source, and in perfumes and medicines. Some Native peoples used this plant to treat irritated mucus membranes, loosen phlegm, induce vomiting, and as a laxative.

Early Blue Violet
Viola adunca

VIOLET FAMIL

A plant of the grasslands and open woods and slopes, this flower blooms early and often in clusters. The flower has purple and white petals, with darker guidelines. The largest petal has a hooked spur half as long as the lower petal. Side petals are white-bearded. The leaves are mostly basal, oval with a heart-shaped base, and the margins have round teeth. The plant grows low to the ground.

Viola is derived from the Latin *violaceous*, for the purple color. *Adunca* means "hooked," a reference to the hook on the spur of the flower. An *uncus* was a hook used by the Romans to drag executed bodies away from the place of execution. Violets have been used for food for centuries. The leaves are high in vitamins A and C and can be used to make a bland tea. Violet seeds have special oily bodies called elaiosomes, which attract ants. The ants carry the seeds away to their nests, thus dispersing the seeds. Common garden Pansies are also a member of the *Viola* genus.

Thread-Leaved Phacelia (Thread-Leaved Scorpionweed)
Phacelia linearis

WATERLEAF FAMILY

This plant appears on dry plateaus and foothills in our area and reaches heights of up to 50 cm. It is an annual species of *Phacelia*. The leaves are hairy, alternate, thin and linear below, developing side lobes higher on the stem. The flowers are reasonably large, lavender to blue and appearing in open clusters from the leaf axils.

The common name, Scorpionweed, most probably arises because some people say the coiled branches of the flower clusters resemble the tail of a scorpion. The genus name, *Phacelia*, is from the Greek *phakelos*, meaning "bundle" or "cluster" a reference to the tightly clustered appearance of the flowers on some members of the genus. The first specimen of the species was collected by Meriwether Lewis in the spring of 1806 near The Dalles, Oregon.

White, Green, and Brown Flowers

This section includes flowers that are predominantly
white or cream-coloured, green, or brown when
encountered in the field. Given that some flowers fade
to other colours as they age, if you do not find the
flower you are looking for in this section, check
the other sections in the book.

Water Calla (Water Arum)
Calla palustris
ARUM -FAMILY

Elaine Nepstad image

This perennial grows up to 20 cm tall from a long, thick rootstock, and occurs in shallow water in wet bogs, sloughs, ditches, and swampy areas. Without question, the distinctive thing about this plant is the large, showy, white, oval bract which wraps around the dense, cylindrical, club-like spike on which the inconspicuous flowers occur. The flower spike is referred to as a spadix, and the bract is referred to as a spathe.

The genus name, *Calla*, is derived from the Greek *kallos*, which means "beautiful." The species name, *palustris*, means "of the marsh," a reference to the preferred habitat of the plant. The plant is related to the plant sold in florist shops as Calla Lily. It has been reported that some Native peoples used the plant as a food source, but other evidence indicates that some people experience a rash-like dermatological reaction when they touch the plant. Apparently the plant contains needle-like crystals of calcium oxalate, the compound that causes kidney stones. This plant is closely related to the familiar Skunk Cabbage (*Lysichitum americanum*), which does not occur in our area, but does occur in many locations in British Columbia.

Evening Star
Mentzelia decapetala
BLAZING STAR FAMILY

Glen Lee image

This stout, leafy, branched biennial grows up to 90 cm tall, and appears on roadsides, exposed clay hillsides, and eroded badlands in the prairie elevation. The leaves are alternate, prominently veined, sharply toothed, up to 15 cm long, and are roughened with thick, whitish, spine-like hairs. The upper leaves are stalkless. The large flowers appear at the terminal ends of the branches. The white flowers are showy, and have 5 sepals and 10 lance- to spatula-shaped, pointed petals, 5 of which are modified sterile stamens (staminodes). There are numerous yellow stamens. The petals are surrounded by hairy, triangular, pale orange bracts that are joined at the base. The flowers open in the evening and bloom during the night, thus the common name Evening Star. The nighttime blooming may be explained by the plant's use of moths as pollinators.

The genus name, *Mentzelia*, honours Christian Mentzel, a 17th-century German botanist. The species name, *decapetala*, means "ten petals." The plant has a variety of locally common names, including Ten Fetal Blazing Star, Ten Petal Mentzelia, and Sand Lily, though the plant is not a member of the Lily Family. Another member of the genus, Blazing Star (*M. laevicaulis*), occurs in similar dry habitats in southern British Columbia. It has very large, showy, yellow flowers.

Clustered Oreocarya
Cryptantha nubigena

BORAGE FAMILY

This plant is densely covered with bristly white hairs, and occurs on dry hillsides and in prairie habitats. The lower leaves are spoon-shaped with rounded to pointed tips, while the upper leaves are linear. The small, white flowers appear in clusters in the axils of the leaves on the upper two-thirds of the erect stem. The pleasantly scented flowers are funnel-shaped, five-parted, and have yellow centres. The flowers bloom early in the spring.

The genus name, *Cryptantha*, is derived from the Greek *kryptos*, which means "hidden," and *anthos*, which means "flower," a reference to some members of the genus that have flowers that never open. The plant is sometimes referred to as Miner's Candle. In California the plant is locally known as Sierra Forget-Me-Not.

Buck-Bean (Bog-Bean)
Menyanthes trifoliata

BUCK-BEAN FAMILY

Margot Hervieux image

This perennial is an aquatic to semi-aquatic plant that grows up to 30 cm tall from a thick, scaly, creeping rootstock. It appears in swampy land, bogs, ditches, and lake and pond margins. The leaves are basal, clasping, long-stemmed, and compound, with 3 smooth, elliptical, shiny, green leaflets. The leafless flowering stems arise from the leaves and hold crowded clusters of white flowers at their ends. The flowers are whitish inside, pink to purplish outside, and have a tube-shaped, five-part corolla, densely bearded inside.

The genus name, *Menyanthes*, is said to originate from the Greek *men*, which means "month," and *anthos*, which means "flower," said to be a reference to the length of time of blooming of the plant. The species name, *trifoliata*, refers to the three-parted leaves. Some Native peoples used the rhizomes of the plant as famine food. They also brewed a tea made from the leaves and used it medicinally for a variety of ailments, including migraine headaches, fevers, and indigestion. The whole plant is also browsed by ungulates. The reference to Bean in the common name is a mystery, this plant bearing no relation whatsoever to beans by way of leaf, flower, or fruit.

Narrow-Leaved Dock
Rumex salicifolius

BUCKWHEAT FAMILY

This plant, and related docks, is a familiar sight in sloughs, roadside ditches, and wet open ground. The plant is erect and may have numerous stems, growing to 60 cm tall. The leaves are alternate, entire, narrowly lance-shaped, tapered at both ends, and often folded at the midline. The greenish flowers are inconspicuous, lack petals, and occur in clusters at the top of the stem.

The genus name, *Rumex*, is the ancient Latin name for Docks and the related Sorrels. The species name, *salicifolius*, means "leaves like willow," and, indeed, another common name for this plant is Willow Dock. Some Native peoples used the plant as a vegetable, and they also employed the plant in poultices. Plants in this genus contain high levels of oxalic acid, which is said to give the plants a lemony flavour. Oxalic acid in low doses is not harmful, but when taken in large doses it interferes with the body's ability to process minerals. A closely related plant, Western Dock (*R. occidentalis*) occurs in similar habitat. It is also known as Indian Rhubarb, and it is related to garden rhubarb. Traditionally, crushed dock leaves have been used as a poultice to treat the sting from nettles.

Water Crowfoot (Water Buttercup)
Ranunculus aquatilis

BUTTERCUP FAMILY

This aquatic Buttercup lives in ponds, lakes, slow-moving streams, and ditches. The white flowers have 5 sepals, 5–10 petals, and numerous pistils and stamens. The plant has two types of leaves. The submerged leaves are thread-like filaments that are matting, and the floating leaves are deeply cleft into 3–5 lobes. The flowers are flecked with gold at the base, and are buoyed above the water's surface on short stems. Yellow Water Crowfoot, which has yellow petals, is now considered to be in the same species. See photograph on the right above.

This plant can occur in abundance, and sometimes covers the surface of small ponds and slow-moving streams. Water Crowfoot is pollinated by insects. The common name, Crowfoot, may originate as a reference to the shape of the floating leaves

Baneberry
Actaea rubra
BUTTERCUP FAMILY

A plant of moist shady woods and thickets, often found along streams. Baneberry is a tall, often branching, thick-stemmed, leafy perennial. The flower is a dense, white, cone-shaped cluster that appears on top of a spike. The fruit is a large cluster of either shiny red or white berries. At the time of flowering, there is no way to determine whether the berries of a particular plant will be red or white.

The common name of the plant is derived from the Anglo-Saxon word *bana*, meaning "murderer" or "destroyer"—undoubtedly a reference to the fact that the leaves, roots, and berries of this plant are extremely poisonous. As few as 2 berries can induce vomiting, bloody diarrhea, and finally, cardiac arrest or respiratory paralysis. The genus name *Actaea* is derived from the Greek *aktaia*, meaning "elder tree," as the leaves are similar to elder leaves. The species name *rubra* is Latin for "red," a reference to the berries. There have been reports of children who have died as a result of eating the berries.

Canada Anemone
Anemone canadensis

BUTTERCUP FAMILY

A plant of moist grasslands and woods, aspen groves, and riverine thickets. The leaves are toothed and deeply divided into 3–5 lobes on long leaf stalks. The leaves are light green, with fine hairs above and below. They are long-veined and attached to the stem in a whorl. The flowers are composed of 5 white petal-like sepals that are rounded at the tip, with soft hairs underneath.

The genus name is said to be derived from the Greek word *anemos*, which means "wind"—most probably a reference to the fact that the wind distributes the long-stemmed fruits of the plant. The whole plant is poisonous and can cause skin irritation if handled, and severe gastroenteritis and ulceration if ingested.

Western Clematis
Clematis ligusticifolia
BUTTERCUP FAMILY

This plant is a climbing or trailing, woody vine that occurs in coulees, creek bottoms, and river valleys. It clings to and climbs over other plants by a twist or kink in its leaf stalks. The leaves are opposite and compound, with 5–7 long-stalked leaflets. The flowers are white, and borne in dense clusters. The flowers are unisexual. The male flowers have many stamens, but no pistils, while the female flowers have both pistils and sterile stamens.

The origin of the genus and common name is explained in the note on Blue Clematis (*C. occidentalis*), shown on page 72. The whole plant is toxic if ingested. Some Native peoples mashed the leaves and branches and used the juices as a headwash. Some Native peoples also boiled the leaves and applied the decoction to boils and sores. Clematis also occurs in yellow (*C. tangutica*) and blue, and often goes by the locally common name of Virgin's Bower. The flowers of these two species are quite different in appearance to Western Clematis. The flowers of these species resemble crepe paper.

Wind Flower
Anemone multifida
BUTTERCUP FAMILY

This plant favours south-facing slopes, grasslands, and open woods. Like all anemones, Wind Flowers possess no petals, only sepals. The flowers are a variety of colours, from white, to yellowish, to red, and appear atop a woolly stem. Beneath the flowers are bract-like leaves attached directly to the stem. The leaves are palmate, with deeply incised, silky-haired leaflets, somewhat reminiscent of poppy leaves. The fruits are achenes in a rounded head, which later form a large cottony mass.

The common name, Wind Flower, comes from the method of distributing the long-plumed seeds of the plant. This flower is also commonly referred to as Cut-Leaved Anemone.

Cow Parsnip
Heracleum lanatum

CARROT FAMILY

A plant of shaded riverine habitat, stream banks, and moist open aspen woods, this plant can attain heights of over 2 m. The flowers are distinctive in large, compound, umbrella-shaped clusters (umbels) composed of numerous white flowers, with white petals in fives. The leaves are compound in threes, usually very large, softly hairy, deeply lobed, and toothed.

Heracleum refers to Hercules, likely because of the plant's large size. Cow Parsnip is also locally known as Indian Celery and Indian Rhubarb. The roots were cooked and eaten by some Native peoples, though there are some sources that say they are poisonous. The Blackfoot roasted the young spring stalks and ate them. They also used the stalks in their Sun Dance ceremony. Caution should be taken to distinguish this plant from the violently poisonous Water Hemlock (*Cicuta maculata*), shown on page 129.

Water Hemlock
Cicuta maculata (also *Cicuta douglasii*)
CARROT FAMILY

A plant of marshes, river and stream banks, and low, wet areas. The plant produces several large umbrella-like clusters (compound umbels) of white flowers appearing at the top of a sturdy stalk. The leaves are alternate, with many bipinnate and tripinnate leaflets that are lance-shaped. The side veins in the leaflets end between the notched teeth on the leaflets, rather than at their points.

The genus name, *Cicuta*, is the Latin name of some poisonous member of the Carrot Family. While lovely to look at, with its umbrella-shaped clusters of flowers on sturdy stems, the Water Hemlock is considered to be perhaps the most poisonous plant in North America. All parts of the plant are poisonous, as testified to by several common names which include Children's Bane, Beaver Poison, and Death of Man. The toxin, cicutoxin, acts on the central nervous system and causes violent convulsions, followed by paralysis and respiratory failure. Some Native peoples used the powdered root as a poison on arrows. If you touch this plant or cut it with an implement for any reason, wash your hands and the implement immediately and thoroughly. A similar plant appears in the same habitat—the Sharptooth Angelica (*Angelica arguta*)—but the leaf veins in Angelica run to the points of the teeth margins on the leaves.

Common Cattail
Typha latifolia
CATTAIL FAMILY

This plant is very common and well recognized from slough and pond margins and along streams in the area. The leaves are long, flat, and strap-like, and the unisexual flowers are cylindrical, dense flower masses. The top of the mass consists of the pollen-bearing male flowers, while the bottom holds the tightly packed pistillate flowers.

Cattails were used extensively by Native peoples. The leaves of the plants were woven into mats, hats, bags, and even capes; the seed heads were used as an absorbent in diapers, as well as for stuffing in mattresses and pillows; the young flowers and rhizomes were eaten. Cattails are also very important cover and food source for a variety of birds and small mammals. Captain William Clark of the Lewis and Clark expedition noted in his journal that members of the expedition had purchased hats and mats made from the plant from natives near the mouth of the Columbia River in late 1805.

Arrow-Leaved Sweet Coltsfoot
Petasites sagittatus
COMPOSITE FAMILY

This plant occurs from low to subalpine elevations in wetlands, ditches, and slough margins, sometimes appearing in standing water. The basal leaves are large, long-stalked, triangular to heart-shaped, have toothed margins, and are densely white-woolly underneath. The flowering stems appear prior to the basal leaves. The stem does not have leaves, but does have some overlapping bracts. The flowers are a torch-like cluster of composite heads with glandular, woolly-hairy bases, sitting atop the stem. The flowers consist almost entirely of whitish disk flowers, sometimes with a few white ray flowers.

The genus name, *Petasites*, is derived from the Greek *petasos*, which means "broad-brimmed hat," a reference to the large leaves. Members of the genus have long been used in herbal medicine to treat coughs, asthma, and colic. The leaves were also used in poultices for wounds and inflammations. The leaves yield a yellowish-green dye. A similar species appears in the same habitat, Palmate Coltsfoot (*P. frigidus*), but it has leaf blades that are palmately lobed into 5–7 sharply toothed segments.

Ox-Eye Daisy
Leucanthemum vulgare

COMPOSITE FAMILY

An invasive Eurasian perennial from a well-developed rhizome, this plant frequents low to mid-elevations in moist to moderately dry sites, such as roadsides, clearings, pastures, and disturbed areas. The flowers are solitary composite heads at the ends of branches, with white ray flowers and yellow disk flowers. The basal leaves are broadly lance-shaped or narrowly spoon-shaped. The stem leaves are oblong and smaller.

Daisy is from the Anglo-Saxon *day's eye*, a reference to the fact that the English daisy closes at night and opens at sun-up. One of the most common and recognizable wildflowers in North America, the Ox-Eye Daisy is very prolific, and will overgrow large areas if not kept in check. A similar flower, Scentless Chamomile (*Matricaria perforata*) occurs in similar habitat and is often confused with Ox-Eye Daisy. To confirm the identity, closely inspect the leaves on the plant. Scentless Chamomile has much thinner leaflets, and they are much more dissected than are those of Ox-Eye Daisy.

Pineapple Weed
Matricaria discoidea

COMPOSITE FAMILY

This branching annual grows up to 40 cm tall along roadsides, in ditches, and on disturbed ground. The stem leaves are alternate and fern-like, with finely dissected, narrow segments. Basal leaves have usually fallen off before flowering occurs. The flowers are several to many composite heads, with greenish to yellow disk florets on a cone-shaped or dome-shaped base. There are no ray florets.

The genus name, *Matricaria*, is derived from the Latin *mater* or *matrix*, meaning "mother" or "womb," and *caria*, meaning "dear," and is a reference to use of the plant in the treatment of uterine infections and other gynecological conditions. When crushed, the leaves and flowers of the plant produce a distinctive pineapple aroma, hence the common name. Some Native peoples used the plant medicinally, while others used the plant to scent their homes and baby cradles, or as an insect repellant. Meriwether Lewis collected a sample of the plant in 1806 while he was with the Nez Perce Indians in Idaho. The plant is also known as Rayless Chamomile. Wild Chamomile (*M. perforata*) has similar leaves to Pineapple Weed, but its flowers resemble Ox-Eye Daisy (*Leucanthemum vulgare*), shown on page 132. Wild Chamomile has been used by herbalists for treatment of a variety of conditions.

Tufted Fleabane
Erigeron caespitosus
COMPOSITE FAMILY

A plant of dry, open places, south-facing slopes, coulees, and eroded
badlands, this small white daisy-like flower can grow in large bunches or
clusters. The ray florets are usually white, but sometimes bluish or pink.
The numerous, narrow petals surround central yellow disk florets. The
basal leaves are grey-green, short, hairy, and lance- or spoon-shaped.
The common name, Fleabane, originates from an ancient belief that bundles
of related species would discourage fleas. The genus name, *Erigeron*, is
derived from the Greek *eri*, meaning "spring," and *geron*, meaning "old man,"
and probably is a reference to the overall hairiness of the species. The species
name, *caespitosus*, means "tufted," and probably refers to the growth habit.
Tufted Fleabane contains a volatile turpentine-like oil, and the liquid from
the boiled roots and leaves was used to treat various ailments, such as
rheumatism, hemorrhoids, and gonorrhea.

Fleabanes are difficult to tell apart, and are often difficult to tell from Asters.
Fleabanes generally have narrower, more numerous ray florets than Asters.
In addition, if you check the involucral bract—the small green cup under
the flower—and see that all of the bracts are the same length, then you have
a Fleabane. If some of the bracts are obviously shorter, you have an Aster.

Yarrow
Achillea millefolium
COMPOSITE FAMILY

A plant of dry to moist grasslands, open riverine forests, aspen woods, and disturbed areas. The individual white flower heads appear in a dense, flat-topped or rounded terminal cluster. The ray florets are white to cream-coloured (sometimes pink), and the central disk florets are straw-coloured. The leaves are woolly, greyish to blue-green, and finely divided, almost appearing to be a fern. Yarrow can occur in large colonies.

The common name is derived from the name of a Scottish parish. The genus name, *Achillea*, is in honour of Achilles, the Greek warrior with the vulnerable heel, who was said to have made an ointment from this plant to heal the wounds of his soldiers during the siege of Troy. The species name, *millefolium*, means "thousand leaves," in reference to the many finely divided leaf segments. Yarrow contains an alkaloid called achillein that reduces the clotting time of blood. It appears a number of Native peoples were aware of this characteristic of the plant, and made a mash of the crushed leaves to wrap around wounds.

Northern Gooseberry
Ribes oxyacanthoides

CURRANT FAMILY

This plant is an erect or sprawling deciduous shrub, growing up to 90 cm tall, which occurs in moist woods, thickets, and open areas. The branches of the plant are covered with small prickles and also have stout spines up to 1 cm long at the branch nodes. The leaves are alternate and shaped like maple leaves, with 3–5 palmate lobes. The flowers are white to greenish-yellow in colour, tubular in shape, have 5 erect petals and 5 larger, spreading sepals, and bloom from the leaf axils in the early spring. The fruits are smooth bluish-purple berries up to 1 cm in diameter.

For an explanation of the genus name, *Ribes*, see the note on Black Gooseberry (*R. lacustre*), shown on page 199. The species name, *oxyacanthoides*, is derived from the Greek *oxys*, which means "pointed," *acantha*, which means "thorn," and *oides*, which means "like." Gooseberries were used by Native peoples as a food source. The spines from the plant were employed as needles. The plant has several locally common names, including Canadian Gooseberry and Inland Gooseberry.

Spreading Dogbane
Apocynum androsaemifolium
DOGBANE FAMILY

A fairly common shrub in thickets and wooded areas, the plant has freely branching, slender stems. The leaves are opposite, egg-shaped, and have sharp pointed tips. The leaves generally droop during the heat of the day. The small, bell-shaped, pink flowers droop from the ends of the leafy stems, usually in clusters. The petal lobes are spreading and bent back, usually with dark pink veins.

The genus name, *Apocynum*, is derived from the Greek *apo*, meaning "against," and *kyon*, meaning "dogs," thus the common name. The pods of the plant are poisonous and it may have been that the pods were used to concoct a poison for dispensing with unwanted dogs. The tough fibers from the stems of Dogbanes were rolled into a strong, fine thread by Native peoples. Several strands plaited together were used for bow strings, and the cord was also used to make fishing nets. When broken, the leaves and stems exude a milky sap. The plant contains a chemical related to digitalis, and was once used as a digitalis substitute, but harmful side effects brought an end to that practice. A similar species, Indian-Hemp Dogbane (*A. cannabinum*) occurs in similar habitat, but it is a generally larger species with small flowers and ascending leaves. The two species can overlap and interbreed, producing an intermediate species known as Western Dogbane (*A. medium*).

Bunchberry (Dwarf Dogwood)
Cornus canadensis

DOGWOOD FAMILY

A plant of moist coniferous woods, often found on rotting logs and stumps. The flowers are clusters of inconspicuous greenish-white flowers, set among 4 white, petal-like showy bracts. The leaves are in a terminal whorl of 4–7, all prominently veined. The leaves are dark green above, lighter underneath. The fruits are bright red berries.

The genus name, *Cornus*, is Latin for "horn" or "antler," possibly a reference to the hard wood of some members of this genus. Another school of thought is that the inflorescence of the plant bears a resemblance to the cornice piece, a knob on cylinders used for rolling up manuscripts. *Canadensis* is a reference to Canada, this plant being widely distributed across the country in the boreal forests. Bunchberry's common name is probably derived from the fact that the fruits are all bunched together in a terminal cluster. A Nootka legend has it that the Bunchberry arose from the blood of a woman marooned in a cedar tree by her jealous husband. The plant is reported to have an explosive pollination mechanism wherein the petals of the mature but unopened flower buds suddenly reflex and the anthers spring out, casting pollen loads into the air. When an insect brushes against the tiny bristle at the end of one petal it triggers this explosion.

Red Osier Dogwood
Cornus stolonifera
DOGWOOD FAMILY

This willow-like shrub that grows up to 3 m high often forms impenetrable thickets along streams and in moist forests. The reddish bark is quite distinctive and becomes even redder with the advent of frosts. The leaves are heavily veined, dark green above and pale underneath. The flowers are small, greenish-white, and occur in a flat-topped cluster at the terminal ends of stems. The fruits are small white berries, appearing in clumps.

The common name, Osier, appears to be from the Old French *osiere*, meaning "that which grows in an osier-bed (streambed)." Native peoples used the branches of the plant to fashion fish traps, poles, and salmon stretchers. This plant is extremely important winter browse for moose.

Gumbo Evening-Primrose (Butte-Primrose)
Oenothera caespitosa

EVENING PRIMROSE FAMILY

Glen Lee image

This low-growing, tufted perennial grows from a woody root and is found on dry clay slopes, eroded prairie, and roadcuts. The leaves are basal, entire, spoon- to lance-shaped, wavy-margined, prominently midveined, and irregularly toothed. They occur in a rosette on the ground, and may have a reddish tinge. The sweet-scented flowers are showy and white, with 4 large, shallowly lobed petals, and 4 sepals that are often reflexed and pale pink. The flowers are short-lived, and become pinker as they age.

The origin of the genus name, *Oenothera*, is explained in the note on Yellow Evening-Primrose (*O. biennis*), shown on page 38. The species name, *caespitosa*, is Latin for "tufted," a reference to the growth habit of the plant. The flower usually opens late in the day and remains open at night, using moths as pollinators. This plant goes by a number of common names, including Tufted Evening-Primrose, Rock Rose, and Gumbo Lily, though it is not a member of the Lily Family.

Wild Sarsaparilla
Aralia nudicaulis
GINSENG FAMILY

This plant prefers the dark woods of the moist montane forests. The leaves are up to 50 cm long, arising singly from an underground stem. Each leaf has a long bare stalk that terminates in 3–5 leaflets each. The leaflets are up to 15 cm long, and are sharply toothed and pointed at the ends. The flowers arise from a short stem near ground level, well below the spreading leaflets. The flowers are tiny, whitish-green, and arranged in 3 round shaped umbels.

The genus name, *Aralia*, is the Latinized form of the French *aralie*, the Quebec Habitant name for the plant. The species name, *nudicaulis*, means "bare stem," a reference to the leafless flower stalk. The plant was used as a stimulant in sweat lodges by some Native peoples, and was also used in a variety of other medicinal ways.

Grass-of-Parnassus
Parnassia palustris

GRASS-OF-PARNASSUS FAMILY

These plants abound in riverine habitat, pond edges, and boggy places. The white flowers are very delicate looking. The flowers appear as singles on a slender stem, with 5 white petals with greenish or yellowish veins. Alternating fertile and sterile stamens are characteristic of this genus. The leaves are mostly basal and broadly kidney-shaped. A single leaf clasps the flowering stem about halfway up.

The name of this plant seems to present some confusion. One school of thought is that the genus name, *Parnassia*, is from Mount Parnassus in Greece, said to be a favourite retreat of the god Apollo. Another school of thought holds that the name comes from a description of the plant written in the first-century by Dioscorides, a military physician for the Emperor Nero. When the description was translated, "grass" was included in the translation and it stuck. There is no doubt that this plant is not even remotely grass-like. A similar species, Fringed Grass-of-Parnassus (*P. fimbriata*) occurs in similar habitat at higher elevations, and it has fringed margins between the petals.

Blueberry (Canada Blueberry)
Vaccinium myrtilloides

HEATH FAMILY

Glen Lee image

This low, deciduous, many-branched shrub grows to heights of 40 cm in dense clumps in dry bogs, coniferous forests, mixed woods, and on rocky ground. It is found coast to coast in Canada. The twigs on the shrub are hairy. The leaves are oval, alternate, softly hairy (particularly underneath), short-stalked, and taper to each end. The flowers are greenish, tinged with pink, urn-shaped, and occur in short clusters. The fruits are light blue berries covered with a whitish film, which are extremely tasty.

The genus name, *Vaccinium*, is said to be derived from the Latin *vacca*, which means "cow," a reference to some berry shrub that cattle once browsed. The species name, *myrtilloides*, is Latin meaning "like those of the myrtle plant," a reference to the similarity of these leaves to those of myrtle bushes. The fruits of the plant can be eaten raw, or made into pies, jams, and syrups. Wild blueberry pancakes are outstanding. Native peoples made extensive use of the berries as a food source. They also used the leaves and fruits medicinally for a variety of ailments. The berries are also relished by bears, various birds, and ungulates.

Bog Cranberry
Vaccinium vitis-idaea

HEATH FAMILY

Margot Hervieux image

This plant is a creeping or trailing, many-branched, mat-forming evergreen dwarf shrub that grows to heights of 10–20 cm in moist places, on open slopes, and on raised areas in bogs, mostly in the northern part of the area. The small leaves are alternate, leathery, and have rolled edges with black dots on the undersides. The flowers are whitish to light pink and urn-shaped, occurring in short clusters at the branch ends. The fruits are red berries that are 5–10 mm in diameter.

The genus name, *Vaccinium*, is the Latin name for Blueberry. The species name, *vitis-idaea*, is derived from the Latin *vitis*, which means "grape vine," and Idaea, who was a nymph in Greek mythology. The plant is sometimes referred to as Lingonberry. Two other locally common names are Cowberry and Foxberry. Low-Bush Cranberry (*Viburnum edule*), shown on page 150, also appears in the area, but it is a member of the Honeysuckle Family and is a substantially different plant. There is another plant known as Bog Cranberry (*V. oxycoccos*), but it usually appears at higher elevations. It has pink nodding flowers, with the petals curved backwards, similar in shape to the Shooting Star (*Dodecatheon pulchellum*), shown on page 111.

144

Greenish-Flowered Wintergreen
Pyrola chlorantha

HEATH FAMILY

An erect perennial that inhabits moist to dry coniferous and mixed forests and riverine environments. The flowers have 5 greenish white, waxy petals and a long style attached to a prominent ovary. The flowers have a bell shape and are distributed on short stalks up the main stem. The leaves are basal in a rosette. The leaves have a leathery appearance and are shiny, rounded, and dark green.

The genus name, *Pyrola*, is derived from Latin *pyrus*, which means "a pear," probably a reference to the leaves being pear-shaped. Wintergreen leaves contain acids that are effective in treating skin irritations. Mashed leaves of *Pyrola* species have traditionally been used by herbalists in skin salves, and poultices for snake and insect bites. They are called wintergreen, not because of the taste, but because the leaves remain green during the winter. Like orchids, these plants require a specific fungus in the soil to grow successfully, and transplantation should not be attempted. Another species of *Pyrola*, Pink Wintergreen (*P. asarifolia*), shown on page 206, is similar in shape and occurs in similar habitat, but has pink flowers.

Indian-Pipe (Ghost Plant)
Monotropa uniflora

HEATH FAMILY

This unique and unusual plant grows either solitary or in clumps from a dense root system, and occurs in moist, shaded poplar woods in rich soil. It is rare, and is said to appear almost overnight, like a mushroom. Instead of leaves, it has colourless scales. The flowers are white to cream-coloured, nodding on stems up to 20 cm tall, and shaped like a smoking pipe stuck into the ground by the stem. The flowers darken to black with age, and turn upward at the top of the stem. Stems from the previous year's growth may persist.

The genus name, *Monotropa*, is derived from the Greek *monos*, meaning "one," and *tropos*, meaning "direction," a reference to the flowers being turned to one side. This plant contains no chlorophyll, and is saprophytic, meaning it obtains its nutrients from dead and decaying plant or animal matter. Native peoples used the plant for a number of medicinal purposes. Other common names applied to the plant are Ghost Flower, Corpse Plant, and Ice Plant. Another member of the genus, Pinesap (*M. hypopithys*) exists in similar habitat, but it is rarer yet. It has light brown to cream-coloured, numerous, urn-shaped flowers on its stem. Pitcher Plant (*Sarracenia purpurea*), shown on page 213, is also referred to locally as Indian Pipe, but it is a different plant altogether.

146

Labrador Tea
Ledum groenlandicum

HEATH FAMILY

This evergreen, much-branched shrub is widespread in low to subalpine elevations in peaty wetlands and moist coniferous forests. The flowers are white and numerous, with 5–10 protruding stamens in umbrella-like clusters at the ends of branches. The leaves are alternate and narrow, with edges rolled under. They are deep green and leathery on top, with dense rusty hairs underneath.

The leaves, used fresh or dried, can be brewed into an aromatic tea, but should be used in moderation to avoid drowsiness. Excessive doses are reported to act as a strong diuretic. The aromatic leaves were used in barns to drive away mice, and in houses to keep away fleas.

One-Sided Wintergreen
Pyrola secunda (also *Orthilia secunda*)

HEATH FAMILY

A small forest dweller that grows to 5–15 cm tall. The white to yellowish-green flowers lie on one side of the arching stalk, arranged in a raceme of 6–10 flowers, sometimes more. The flowers resemble small street lights strung along a curving pole. The straight style sticks out beyond the petals, with a flat, five-lobed stigma. The leaves are basal, egg-shaped, and finely toothed at the margins.

One-Sided Wintergreen is included in the *Pyrola* genus by some taxonomists, but is put into the *Orthilia* genus by others. *Orthilia* is derived from the Greek *orthos*, meaning "straight," most probably a reference to the straight style. The species name, *secunda*, is derived from the Latin *secundus*, meaning "next" or "following," a reference to the flowers which follow each other on the same side of the stem. Once seen, this delightful little flower is unmistakable in the woods.

Single Delight
Moneses uniflora (also *Pyrola uniflora*)

HEATH FAMILY

This delightful little forest dweller is also known as One-Flowered Wintergreen, and it inhabits damp forests, usually on rotting wood. The plant is quite tiny, standing only 10 cm tall, and the single white flower, open and nodding at the top of the stem, is less than 5 cm in diameter. The flower looks like a small white umbrella offering shade. The leaves are basal, oval, and evergreen, attached to the base of the stem. The style is prominent and tipped with a five-lobed stigma, which almost looks like a mechanical part of some kind.

The genus name, *Moneses*, is derived from the Greek *monos*, meaning "solitary," and *hesia*, meaning "delight," a reference to the delightful single flower. Other common names include Wood Nymph and Shy Maiden. In Greek mythology, nymphs were nature goddesses, beautiful maidens living in rivers, woods, and mountains, and once you see this diminutive flower, the common names seem completely appropriate.

Low-Bush Cranberry (Mooseberry)
Viburnum edule
HONEYSUCKLE FAMILY

This plant is a sprawling deciduous shrub that grows to heights of up to 2 m, from low to subalpine elevations in moist to wet forests, along streams, and in boggy areas. The leaves are opposite, sharply toothed, and maple-leaf shaped with 3 lobes. The tiny, white, five-parted flowers appear in flat-topped showy clusters between leaves along the stem. The fruits are clusters of red or orange berries that contain a large, flattened stone. The fruits remain on the plant after the leaves fall, and the over-ripe berries and decaying leaves often produce a musty odour in the woods near the plants.

The species name, *edule*, means "edible," and refers to the fruits of the plant. The fruits are favoured by birds. The fruits were used extensively by Native peoples as a food source, and other parts of the plant were used medicinally. In the fall, the leaves of this plant turn beautiful crimson and purple colours. Two other locally common names for the plant are Mooseberry and Squash-berry. Some confusion can arise because of the existence of a plant called a High-Bush Cranberry (*V. trilobum*), which occurs in similar habitat. That plant is a larger bush—almost a small tree—with similar flowers and fruits. Neither the Low-Bush or the High-Bush are truly Cranberries, which are members of the Heath Family. There is another plant in the area that is a Cranberry—the Bog Cranberry (*Vaccinium vitis-idaea*), shown on page 144.

Snowberry
Symphoricarpos albus
HONEYSUCKLE FAMILY

This common deciduous shrub occurs from coast to coast in North America, and is found from prairies to lower subalpine zones, in well-drained, open or wooded sites. There are several subspecies that are so alike it requires dissection and magnification to tell one from the other. The shrub is erect, and can attain heights of 2 m. The branches are opposite and slender, and, on close examination, covered with tiny hairs. The leaves are opposite, elliptic to oval, and pale green. The flowers are white to pink, and broadly funnel-shaped, occurring in clusters at the ends of the twigs. The stamens and style do not protrude from the flower. The fruits are waxy, white berry-like drupes that occur in clusters, and often persist through the winter.

The berries of this plant were not eaten by Native peoples, and many considered them poisonous. In fact, some Indians called the berries Corpse Berries and Ghost Berries. Some Native peoples believed that these white berries were the ghosts of Saskatoon berries, and thus part of the spirit world and not to be tampered with by the living.

Twinflower
Linnaea borealis
HONEYSUCKLE FAMILY

This small trailing evergreen is common in coniferous forests, but easily overlooked by the casual observer. This plant sends runners creeping over the forest floor, over mosses, fallen logs, and stumps. At frequent intervals the runners give rise to the distinctive "Y" shaped stems, 5–10 cm tall. Each fork of the stem supports at its end a slightly flared, pink to white, trumpet-like flower that hangs down like a small lantern on a tiny lamppost. The flowers have a sweet perfume that is most evident near evening.

The genus name, *Linnaea*, honours Carolus Linnaeus, the Swedish botanist who is the father of modern plant nomenclature. It is said that this flower was his favourite among the thousands of plants he knew. The species name, *borealis*, means "northern," referring to the circumpolar northern habitat of the plant. Some Native peoples made a tea from the leaves of this plant.

Carrion Flower
Smilax herbacea
LILY FAMILY

Glen Lee image

This plant inhabits shady, moist woods and river valleys in the central and eastern prairies, and blooms in the spring or early summer. It is a thornless vine that clings to fences, trees, and bushes by slender tendrils that emerge from the leaf axils. The plant can grow to lengths of over 2 m. The plant is dioecious, meaning that each plant has unisex flowers, with the male and female flowers blooming on separate plants. The flowers are greenish-white compound umbels that emerge along the stem. The common name comes from the odour of rotten flesh that emanates from the plant, attracting flies as pollinators.

The genus name, *Smilax*, is derived from Greek and means "rasping," referring to the thorns found on most plants in the genus. The species name, *herbacea*, is Latin and means "non-woody," the reference being that this plant is alone in the genus in not having woody stems. Native peoples roasted the tubers as a food source, and also ground them to make flour for baking. The female flowers turn into blue-black berries that are eaten by birds and small mammals.

Death Camas
Zigadenus venenosus

LILY FAMILY

This plant of moist grasslands, grassy slopes, and open woods grows from an onion-like bulb that has no oniony smell. The leaves are mainly basal and resemble grass, with prominent midveins. The greenish-white, foul-smelling flowers appear in tight clusters atop an erect stem, each flower having 3 virtually identical petals and sepals. There are yellowish-green V-shaped glands (nectaries) near the base of the petals and sepals.

The genus name, *Zigadenus*, is derived from the Greek *zygos*, meaning "yoke," and *aden*, meaning "gland," a reference to the shape of the nectary at the base of each petal and sepal. The species name, *venenosus*, is Latin for "very poisonous." Death Camas contains poisonous alkaloids, and is probably even more toxic than its close relative, White Camas (*Z. elegans*), which appears in the same general habitat, but blooms later. These plants have been responsible for killing many people and animals. When the flowers are missing, Death Camas and White Camas are difficult to distinguish from Blue Camas (*Camassia quamash*), another lily, the bulb of which was commonly used as a food source by Native peoples and early settlers.

Fairybells
Disporum trachycarpum

LILY FAMILY

A plant of shaded poplar woods, stream banks, and riverine environments, this delightful flower blooms in early summer. The flowers are bell-shaped, creamy white, and occur in drooping pairs at the end of branches. The leaves of the plant are generally lance-shaped with pointed ends. The fruits are red egg-shaped berries, occurring in pairs.

The genus name, *Disporum*, is derived from the Greek *dis*, meaning "double," and *spora*, meaning "seeds." The species name, *trachycarpum*, means "rough fruited." The berries from Fairybells are edible, but said to be bland. They are a favoured food of many rodents and birds.

False Solomon's-Seal
Smilacina racemosa

LILY FAMILY

A lily of moist woods, rivers and stream banks, thickets and meadows, that can grow up to half a metre tall. The flowers are small and white, arranged in a branching panicle that is upright at the end of the stem. The leaves are broadly lance-shaped, numerous and alternate, gradually tapering to a pointed tip, with prominent parallel veining, sometimes folded at the midline. The fruit is a red berry flecked with maroon.

The genus name, *Smilacina*, means "a small Smilax," and refers to this plant's resemblance to plants in the genus *Smilax*. The species name, *racemosa*, indicates that the plant has a raceme arrangement for the flowers. This name is somewhat confusing in that a raceme is an unbranched cluster of flowers on a common stalk. The flower arrangement on this plant is more precisely referred to as a panicle—a branched flower cluster that blooms from the bottom up. A very similar plant lives in the same habitat—the Star Flowered Solomon's-Seal (*S. stellata*), but it has significantly fewer flowers, which are shaped like six-sided stars. The fruits of Star Flowered Solomon's Seal are cream coloured berries with maroon or brown stripes.

Prairie Onion
Allium textile
LILY FAMILY

This onion is common in sandy soils on dry prairie meadows, hillsides, and coulees, and is said to be the most abundant of the wild onions. The stems are narrow, grooved, and circular, and produce a strong odour of onion if crushed. Several stems can arise from the same bulb. The flowers are numerous, small, and white, borne in a tight upright umbel on the top of the stem. This onion usually blooms earlier than other wild onions.

Native peoples gathered the bulbs and ate them raw, cooked, and in stews and soups. Prairie Onion was also employed as a repellant for moths and insects. Ground squirrels and other small mammals also use this plant in their diets. *Allium* is the Latin name for "garlic," from the Celtic *all*, meaning "hot" or "burning," because it irritates the eyes. The species name, *textile*, is derived from Latin and means "woven," a reference to the intricately intertwined fibres that cover the bulb.

White Camas
Zigadenus elegans

LILY FAMILY

This plant of moist grasslands, grassy slopes, and open woods grows from an onion-like bulb that has no oniony smell. The greenish-white foul-smelling flowers appear in open clusters along an erect stem. There are yellowish-green V-shaped glands (nectaries) near the base of the petals and sepals. The leaves are mainly basal and resemble grass, with prominent midveins.

The origin of the genus name, *Zigadenus* is explained in the narrative on Death Camas (*Z. venenosus*), shown on page 154. The species name, *elegans*, means "elegant." Though elegant indeed, these plants are extremely poisonous, containing very toxic alkaloids, particularly in the bulbs. These plants have been responsible for killing many people and animals. When the flowers are missing, White Camas and the closely related species, Death Camas, are difficult to distinguish from Blue Camas (*Camassia quamash*), another lily, the bulb of which was commonly used as a food source by Native peoples and early settlers. Other common names for White Camas include Mountain Death Camas, Green Lily, and Showy Death Camas.

Northern Bedstraw
Galium boreale

MADDER FAMILY

A plant common to roadsides and woodlands in the montane to subalpine zones. The flowers are tiny, fragrant, and white, occurring in dense clusters at the top of the stems. The individual flowers are cruciform (cross-shaped), with each having 4 spreading petals that are joined at the base. There are no sepals. The smooth stems are square in cross-section, and bear whorls of 4 narrow, lance-shaped leaves, each with 3 veins.

The common name for this plant is a reference to a practice of Native peoples to use the dried, sweet-smelling plants to stuff mattresses. The roots of the plants were a source of red and yellow dyes. The genus name, *Galium*, is derived from the Greek *gala*, which means "milk," a reference to the fact that country folk used to use the juice of another similar plant to curdle milk. The species name, *boreale*, means "northern," a reference to the distribution of the plant worldwide.

Sweet-Scented Bedstraw
Galium triflorum

MADDER FAMILY

This plant occurs in moist mountain forests, along stream banks, and in dense, damp woods. It is a low, trailing perennial that has leaves in whorls of 6, radiating from a common centre stem. The leaves are tipped with a sharp point, and give off a sweet aroma, variously compared to vanilla or cinnamon. The flowers are small, greenish-white, and occur in groups of 3 in the leaf axils, with 4 petals per flower.

The common name, Bedstraw, is derived from the practice of some Native peoples of using the plant for stuffing their mattresses. Another member of the genus, Northern Bedstraw (*G. boreale*), occurs in similar habitat, and was used in the same fashion.

Seneca Snakeroot
Polygala senega
MILKWORT FAMILY

This several-stemmed, unbranched, erect perennial grows up to 50 cm tall from a woody, twisted, rootstalk that has a snake-like appearance, and smells and tastes somewhat like oil of wintergreen. The plant appears in open woods and prairie parklands. The numerous leaves are alternate, narrowly lance-shaped, simple, and up to 30 cm long. The small, numerous flowers are greenish-white, and appear in dense, tapered clusters atop the stems.

The genus name, *Polygala*, is derived from the Greek *poly*, meaning "much" or "many," and *gala*, meaning "milk," a reference to the belief that these plants would enhance milk production. The species name, *senega*, refers to the Seneca Indians. The common name originates from the practice of using the plant to treat snakebite. This plant has historically been touted as a cure for a variety of illnesses, including pleurisy, pneumonia, earaches, toothaches, croup, colds, and gout. It is used today as an expectorant in cough syrups and lozenges. A related plant, Fringed Milkwort (*P. paucifolia*), occurs on the prairies, but is somewhat rare. It is a low-growing species, and has lovely pink to rose-purple flowers.

Morning Glory
Calystegia sepium (also *Convolvulus sepium*)

MORNING GLORY FAMILY

Morning Glory is a twining, climbing, or trailing vine that grows from slender, spreading rhizomes. The flowers are 3–6 cm across, white to pinkish in colour, and trumpet- or funnel-shaped. The leaves are alternate and arrowhead-shaped, and the flowers appear solitary in the leaf axils. The flowers usually close when it is dark, overcast, or raining.

The genus name, *Calystegia*, is derived from the Greek *kalyx*, meaning "cup," and *stegos*, meaning "cover," a reference to the bracts that cover the sepals on the flower. This plant is also commonly called Hedge Bindweed, Lady's Nightcap and Bell-Bind. A closely related plant, Field Bindweed, is a noxious weed that creeps over crops and covers everything within its reach. Unlike many climbing plants, the Bindweeds cannot support their stems and tendrils, so they wind their stems tightly around available supports. Under favourable conditions, a Bindweed stem will complete an encirclement of a support in less than 2 hours time.

Pennycress (Stinkweed)
Thlaspi arvense

MUSTARD FAMILY

This member of the Mustard Family was introduced from Eurasia, and appears at low to mid-elevations in cultivated areas and waste places. It blooms continuously from early spring until frosts arrive. The leaves have irregularly toothed margins, and clasp the stalk. The four-petaled white flowers appear in rounded clusters (racemes) at the tops of the stem.

The genus name, *Thlaspi*, is derived from the Greek *thlao*, which means "to compress," a reference to the fruits of the plant. The species name, *arvense*, means "of cultivated fields." The fruits of Pennycress are flat, circular pods with wide wings around the edges, and a notch at the top. The common name is derived from the resemblance of the fruits to the size of pennies. The plant has a strong, somewhat offensive odour when crushed, thus giving rise to another common name—Stinkweed.

Black Henbane
Hyoscyamus niger

NIGHTSHADE FAMILY

These plants are imports from Europe that are looked upon as a noxious weed. The plant is a biennial and grows to about a metre high. It has large, irregularly shaped, robust leaves. The flowers are bell-shaped and formed in crowded, one-sided spikes near the top of the plant. The petals of the flowers have a distinctive and conspicuous network of purple veins, both inside and outside the petals. The markings on the flowers resemble old, cracked paint. The flowers mature to a capsule that contains many seeds, and resembles a peanut in shape and texture.

Black Henbane contains a number of poisonous alkaloids that are the same as those produced by Bella Donna, including atropine and scopolamine. During the Middle Ages this plant was used in brewing beer to augment the inebriating properties of the product. That practice was eventually abandoned owing to a number of poisonings. Henbane is grown commercially today, and its alkaloids are applied in modern medicine in the production of painkillers and anti-spasmodic drugs.

Hooded Ladies' Tresses
Spiranthes romanzoffiana

ORCHID FAMILY

This orchid is reasonably common in swampy places, meadows, open shady woods, and lakeshores, and can stand up to 60 cm high. The characteristic feature of the plant is the crowded flower spike, which can contain up to 60 densely spaced white flowers that appear to coil around the end of the stem in 3 spiraling ranks. When newly bloomed, the flower has a wonderful aroma, which most people say smells like vanilla.

The common name of the plant is a reference to the braid-like appearance of the flowers, similar to a braid in a lady's hair. The genus name is derived from the Greek *speira*, meaning "coil," and *anthos*, meaning "flower," referring to the spiral inflorescence. The species name honours Russian Count Nicholas Romanzoff, a 19th-century Russian minister of state and patron of science. The species was first discovered on the Aleutian island of Unalaska, when Alaska was still a Russian territory.

Round-Leaved Orchid
Orchis rotundifolia
ORCHID FAMILY

This tiny orchid, standing no more than 25 cm tall, occurs in well-drained parts of bogs and swamps, and in cold, moist, mossy coniferous forests. The flowers are irregular, with 3 white to pink sepals. The upper sepal combines with the upper 2 purple-veined petals to form a hood. The 2 lateral sepals are wing-like. The lowest petal forms a white to pink, oblong lip, spotted with dark red or purple spots. The leaves are basal, solitary, and broadly elliptic.

The genus name is derived from the Greek *orchis*, meaning "testicle," because the swollen tubers of some species resemble testicles. As a result of this, orchids were once thought to be a powerful aphrodisiac for both people and animals. The species name, *rotundifolia*, is Latin meaning "round leafed."

Sparrow's-Egg Lady's Slipper (Franklin's Lady's Slipper)
Cypripedium passerinum

ORCHID FAMILY

This lovely orchid grows from a cord-like rhizome in boggy areas, along streams, and in mossy coniferous areas. It resembles Yellow Lady's Slipper (*C. parviflorum*) in shape, but this flower is smaller, has bright purple dots on the interior, and has shorter, stubbier, greenish sepals. Both the stem and the leaves of the plant are covered in soft hairs.

The origin of the genus name is explained in the note on Yellow Lady's Slipper, shown on page 50. The species name, *passerinum*, means "sparrow-like," a reference to the spotting on the flower being like the markings on a sparrow egg. Care should be taken when moving around these orchids. They are fragile and easily damaged. Picking the flower is anathema—the flower will quickly wilt, and the plant will die without the nutrition provided by the flower.

Ground-Plum
Astragalus crassicarpus

PEA FAMILY

This hardy perennial grows in open prairie and on grassy hillsides, and sprawls over the ground, sometimes forming dense mats up to 1 m in diameter. The stems are decumbent—lying on the ground, with tips ascending—and the inflorescence appears in a loose raceme of 8–10 pea-like flowers at the tip of the stems. The flowers are whitish, with the keel fringed in purple. The fruits are nearly round pods, up to 12 mm in diameter, which are reddish and lie on the ground like small, red plums. The pods give the plant its common name.

The origin of the genus name is discussed in the narrative on Two-Grooved Milk-Vetch (*A. bisulcatus*), shown on page 110. The young pods were eaten, raw or boiled, by some Native peoples. The roots were boiled and used as a toothpaste and treatment for insect bites. The dried, powdered roots were used as a coagulant to stop bleeding. The plant was first described for science by renowned 19th-century English botanist Thomas Nuttall, when he visited the Mandan tribe in the Dakotas in 1810. The plant is occasionally referred to as Buffalo Bean, but should not be confused with Golden Bean (*Thermopsis rhombifolia*), another member of the Pea Family that also goes by the name Buffalo Bean.

White Clover (Dutch Clover)
Trifolium repens

PEA FAMILY

This common plant was introduced from Eurasia for hay, pasture, and soil improvement—it being a nitrogen fixer in the soil. The leaves are composed of 3 leaflets—occasionally 4, if you are lucky—and creep along the ground. The flowers are white and clustered on short, slender stalks in round heads. On close examination the flower cluster is quite intricate in shape, and worthy of close examination.

The name Clover originates from the Latin *clava*, meaning the three-headed weapon carried by Hercules. That same reference is seen in playing cards, in the suit called clubs. Historically, the flowers have been used to flavour cheese and tobacco, and have even been used in famine time to make bread.

White Peavine
Lathyrus ochroleucus

PEA FAMILY

A plant of moist shaded woods and thicket edges, this twining perennial has coiled tendrils at the ends of the leaves, and it climbs on adjacent plants. The flowers are pale yellow to white, and pea-like.

Lathyrus is from the ancient Greek name for a plant like this, or some other member of the Pea Family. The species name, *ochroleucus*, is Greek, meaning "yellowish white," alluding to the flower colour. There is also a purple flowered Peavine in the same habitat (*L. venosus*). The peavines are distinguished from the vetches by their larger leaves and stipules.

Wild Licorice
Glycyrrhiza lepidota
PEA FAMILY

This coarse perennial grows up to 100 cm tall from a thick rootstock that has a slight licorice flavour, and occurs in moist grasslands, along stream and riverbanks, in slough margins, and disturbed areas. The leaves are alternate and pinnately compound, with 11–19 pale green, sharply pointed, lance-shaped leaflets. The leaflets have glandular dots on the underside and produce a lemony odour when crushed. The flowers are yellowish-white, numerous, showy, and occur in dense clusters at the top of the stem. The flowers are typically members of the Pea Family, and have an upward pointing standard that encloses the wings and keel. The flower cluster blooms from the bottom up. The fruits are densely clustered, oblong, flattened reddish pods that are covered with hooked barbs.

The genus name, *Glycyrrhiza*, is derived from the Greek *glykrrhiza*, which means "sweet root." The species name, *lepidota*, means "with small, rough scales," and refers to the glands on the underside of the leaves. Native peoples roasted and ate the roots of the plant, and also used it medicinally to treat a variety of ailments.

Moss Phlox
Phlox hoodii

PHLOX FAMILY

A plant of dry, exposed hillsides, eroded slopes, foothills, and prairies. The small five-petaled flowers with orange stamens are united into a tube below. The leaves are awl-shaped with spiny tips, tiny and overlapping, grey-green, and woolly at the base. The plant grows low to the ground and covers the ground like a moss. The flowers show a tremendous variance in colour, from white to all shades of blue and purple.

The genus name, *Phlox*, is Greek for "flame." The species name, *hoodii*, honours Robert Hood, a midshipman on one of Sir John Franklin's expeditions. This flower blooms early in the spring and adds a wonderful spectrum of colour to an otherwise drab landscape.

Field Chickweed (Mouse-Ear Chickweed)
Cerastium arvense

PINK FAMILY

This early-blooming plant thrives in dry grasslands and rocky and disturbed ground, often forming large mats of white flowers in the spring. The white flowers appear in loose clusters, often many flowers to each plant. The 5 white petals are notched and have green lines on them as nectar guides for insects.

The upper part of the leaf resembles a mouse's ear, thus the common name for the plant. The genus name, *Cerastium*, is derived from the Greek *keras*, meaning "horn," a reference to the shape of the seed capsule. The species name, *arvense*, means "field."

Night-Flowering Catchfly
Silene noctiflora

PINK FAMILY

This plant was introduced from Europe and has become a common and troublesome noxious weed in the prairies. It is an erect, branching plant that grows up to 90 cm tall in ditches, waste areas, and field edges. The leaves, stems, and flowers are sticky and hairy. The leaves are opposite, dark green, and lance-shaped. The flowers are white and fragrant, with the sepals united to form a sticky, oval, tubular, swollen calyx that is up to 2 cm long and handsomely striped with white and green. The 5 petals are deeply cleft at the ends. The flowers open in the evening to attract moths and other night-flying insects, and then close in the morning.

The genus name, *Silene*, is derived from the Greek *sialon*, which means "saliva," a reference to the sticky, glandular hairs on the plant. Those sticky hairs probably also give rise to the common name Catchfly. The species name, *noctiflora*, reflects the habit of the flowers to open only at night. This plant can be confused with White Cockle (*Lychnis alba*), which also occurs in the same habitat and has similarly constructed flowers. White Cockle is not sticky when squeezed.

Mealy Primrose
Primula incana
PRIMROSE FAMILY

A plant of moist meadows and slopes, slough margins, and lake margins, these plants grow low to the ground with a basal rosette of leaves. The flowers are pale purple to white, with yellow centres. The petals are deeply notched and appear at the end of a tubular calyx.

The common name refers to the cream-coloured, mealy scales on the undersides of the leaves. *Primula* is derived from the Latin *primus*, meaning "first," a reference to the early blooming time of many in the genus. The species name, *incana*, is Latin for "pale grey or hoary."

Western Spring Beauty
Claytonia lanceolata

PURSLANE FAMILY

The flowers of this early-blooming plant are white, but may appear pink, owing to the reddish veins in the petals and the pink anthers. The tips of the petals are distinctly notched. The plants are usually less than 20 cm tall, and the flowers appear in loose, terminal short-stalked clusters.

The genus name, *Claytonia*, honours John Clayton, a 17th-century botanist who collected plants in what was to become the United States. The species name, *lanceolata*, refers to the lance-shaped leaves. The Western Spring Beauty was used by Native peoples as food. Bears and rodents also make use of the corms of the plant for food. Ungulates often eat the flowers and leaves. Alpine Spring Beauty (*C. megarhiza*) is a relatively rare, but similar plant that occurs in the alpine zone. It has spoon-shaped, reddish-green, basal leaves.

Birch-Leaf Spirea
Spiraea betulifolia
ROSE FAMILY

This deciduous shrub grows to heights of 70 cm, and occurs in moist to dry, open and wooded sites from valley floors to the subalpine zone. It spreads by underground runners, and often forms dense cover on the forest floor. The plant is alternately branched, with cinnamon-brown bark, and alternate oval- or egg-shaped leaves that are irregularly coarse-toothed towards the tip. The flowers are dull white, often tinged to purple or pink, saucer-shaped, and occurring in flat-topped clusters on the ends of the stems.

The genus name, *Spiraea*, is derived from the Greek *speira*, meaning "spire" or "wreath," possibly a reference to the plant being used as a garland. The species name, *betulifolia*, means "leaves like a birch," the reference being to the similarity of Spirea leaves to those of birch trees. Another common name for the plant is White Meadowsweet. Native peoples and herbalists have long used the plant to relieve pain, reduce inflammations, and treat a variety of other ailments from heartburn to abdominal and menstrual pains. The branches of the plant were also used for drying and smoking fish.

Black Hawthorn
Crataegus douglasii
ROSE FAMILY

This is a large deciduous shrub that can reach up to 8 m in height. The bark is grey, rough, and scaly, and the plant has sharp, stout thorns up to 3 cm long that will command immediate attention from the unwary passerby who stumbles into the plant. The leaves are oval-shaped and appear leathery, with multiple lobes at the top. The flowers are white, showy, and saucer-shaped, occurring in clusters at the tips of the branches. The berries are generally unpalatable dark purplish pomes that contain a large, hard seed.

The genus name, *Crataegus*, is derived from the Greek *kratos*, meaning "strength," a reference to the hard, fine-grained wood of the plant. The common name is derived from the Anglo-Saxon word *haguthorn*, which was "a fence with thorns," referring to the use of this plant as a hedge. Native peoples used the thorns from the plant for various purposes, including probing blisters and boils, fish hooks, and piercing ears. The wood of the plant was used for making tool and weapon handles. The bark from the plant was used medicinally by some Native peoples for treatment of diarrhea and stomach pains. Modern herbalists value Hawthorn berries as a tonic for the treatment of high blood pressure.

Chokecherry
Prunus virginiana

ROSE FAMILY

This plant is a conspicuous white-flowering shrub or small tree that is common in thickets, open woods, and along streams. The five-petaled saucer-shaped flowers are borne in thick cylindrical clusters. The fruit is a red-purple to black berry that is almost all pit. The fruit appears in dense clusters at the terminal ends of branches.

Most people find the fruit of the Chokecherry too bitter to eat raw, thus the common name. The fruits can be processed to produce quite acceptable jelly, syrup, and wine. Birds and mammals seem to relish the fruits. Bears are often drawn to large congregations of Chokecherries and will work over the bushes until the Chokecherries are gone. Ungulates, like elk and deer, forage on the leaves and twigs of the plant.

Pin Cherry
Prunus pensylvanica

ROSE FAMILY

This plant is a deciduous shrub or small tree that can reach up to 5 m in height. The branches are a glossy, reddish-brown, with prominent, raised horizontal slits, which are actually pores that are referred to as "lenticels." The leaves are alternate, lance-shaped, with fine teeth, and tapering to a point at the tip. The white flowers occur in clusters along the branches. Each flower has 5 rounded petals, and is saucer-shaped. The fruits are bright red berries which hang in small clusters.

All portions of this plant except the flesh of the berries contain poisonous hydrocyanic acid, and can cause poisoning. That includes the bark, leaves, wood, and pits contained in the fruit. The fruit is edible, but the pits must be discarded. Birds apparently relish the fruits, and some people refer to the plant as Bird Cherry.

Saskatoon (Serviceberry)
Amelanchier alnifolia

ROSE FAMILY

This deciduous shrub grows to heights of up to 5 m or more, and is found in open woods, on stream banks, and hillsides, from the prairie to montane elevations. The shrub is erect to spreading, with smooth bark that is reddish when new, turning greyish with age. The leaves are alternate, oval to round in shape, rounded at the tips, and coarsely toothed on the upper half. The white flowers are star-shaped, with 5 slender petals, about 2 cm across, and occur in clusters near the branch tips. The petals are wider above the middle, and taper to a slender base. The fruits are sweet and juicy berry-like pomes—like tiny apples—purple to black when ripe.

Saskatoon berries were one of the most important berries for Native peoples. They were eaten fresh or were dried for later use. They were also mashed and dried into large cakes. The Lewis and Clark expedition reported some of these cakes weighed as much as 7 kg. The dried fruits were often added to meats, soups, and stews. The hard, straight branches of the plant were also used for manufacturing arrow shafts, basket rims, canoe parts, and tepee stakes and closures. The plants are also important browse for elk, moose, and deer, and the berries are eaten by bears, small mammals, and birds. During the Great Depression, the Saskatoon was the only fruit known to thousands of prairie dwellers. Other common names for the plant include Juneberry, Serviceberry, and Shadbush.

Trailing Raspberry
Rubus pubescens

ROSE FAMILY

This dwarf shrub is a low, trailing plant with slender runners and erect flowering stems that grows at low to mid-elevations in moist to wet forests and clearings. The plant has soft hairs on it, but no prickles like Wild Red Raspberry (*R. idaeus*). The leaves are palmately divided into 3 oval or diamond-shaped leaflets, with pointed tips and toothed margins. The flowers are white and spreading, and occur on short erect branches. The fruits are red drupelets—the aggregate cluster makes up a raspberry.

Native peoples used this plant as a food source and for medicinal purposes, similarly to Wild Red Raspberry (*R. idaeus*), shown on page 184. Trailing Raspberry is sometimes referred to as Dewberry.

White Cinquefoil
Potentilla arguta

ROSE FAMILY

This species of Cinquefoil is tall—up to 100 cm—and bears creamy white flowers with yellow centres in a compact flower arrangement. It is a glandular-hairy plant that appears in grasslands and meadows. The leaves are bright green, pinnately compound. The basal leaves have 7–11 toothed, hairy leaflets. The upper leaves have 3–5 leaflets.

The genus name, *Potentilla*, is derived from the Latin *potens*, meaning "powerful," most probably a reference to the potent medicinal properties of some of the herbs in the genus. Potentillas have a high tannin content, making them astringent and anti-inflammatory. Herbalists use the plants in the genus for a wide variety of conditions.

Wild Red Raspberry
Rubus idaeus

ROSE FAMILY

This erect to spreading deciduous shrub grows up to 2 m tall at low to subalpine elevations in clearings, along streams, and in disturbed areas. It is similar to cultivated raspberry in appearance. The prickly branches (or canes) are biennial, and are green in the first year, and yellowish brown to cinnamon brown in the second. The leaves are palmately divided (i.e. divided into leaflets that diverge from a common point) into 3–5 egg-shaped, pointed, double saw-toothed leaflets. The flowers are white and drooping, occurring singly or in small clusters. The fruits are juicy red drupelets—a drupelet being one part of an aggregate fruit—in dense clusters, the totality of which is the raspberry. Other examples of fruits that appear as drupelets include blackberries and thimbleberries.

Native peoples made extensive use of Wild Red Raspberries as a food source and for medicinal purposes. A tea brewed from the plant was administered to women to ease the pain of childbirth, and the concoction was also used to treat a variety of other conditions, such as boils, bladder infections, liver problems, and diarrhea. Modern herbalists also value this plant for a variety of conditions. Pharmacologists have validated raspberry leaf as an antispasmodic.

Wild Strawberry
Fragaria virginiana
ROSE FAMILY

A plant of shaded to open gravelly soils and thickets from prairie to alpine habitats. The single five-petaled white flower appears on a leafless stem that is usually shorter than the leaves are long. The stamens are numerous and yellow. The leaves are rounded to broadly oval, toothed, with 3 leaflets on short stalks. The fruit is a red berry, covered with sunken, seed-like achenes. New plants are often established from reddish runners.

Strawberry is said to come from the Anglo-Saxon name *streowberie* because the runners from the plant are strewn across the ground. The genus name, *Fragaria*, means "fragrance." Strawberry plants are rich in iron, calcium, potassium, sodium, and vitamin C. The fruits are delicious, with a more pronounced flavour than domestic strawberries. The leaves have been used to make tea, and have also been used for medicinal purposes.

Pale Comandra (Bastard Toadflax)
Comandra umbellata

SANDALWOOD FAMILY

This erect, blue-green perennial is common in open pine woods, gravel slopes, and grasslands, and springs from a creeping rootstock. The leaves are lance-shaped, and hug the erect stem. The flowers occur in a rounded or flat-topped cluster atop the stem. Each flower is greenish-white, with the sepals separated above, and fused into a small funnel below.

The genus name, *Comandra*, is derived from the Greek *kome*, meaning "hair," and *andros*, meaning "man," probably a reference to the hairy bases of the stamens on the flower. The species name, *umbellata*, is a reference to the shape of the cluster of flowers. The plant has another common name—Bastard Toadflax—though the plant bears no relationship to Toadflax and is not in any way similar. Pale Comandra is a parasite, taking water, and perhaps food, from its host plant.

Richardson's Alumroot
Heuchera richardsonii

SAXIFRAGE FAMILY

This is an erect perennial herb that grows up to 40 cm tall in sandy, gravelly grassland, rocky slopes, and along streams. The long-stemmed leaves are all basal, round to heart-shaped, leathery, lobed, and sharply toothed. The numerous flowers are glandular-hairy, purple to pinkish, and appear in a spiral around the top of tall, leafless, flower stalk.

The genus name, *Heuchera*, honours Dr. Johann von Heucher, a German physician and professor. The species name, *richardsonii*, honours the explorer Sir John Richardson. The common name, Alumroot, is a reference to the alum-like astringent found in the root of the plant. Native peoples used the plant medicinally for a variety of ailments. A similar species, Round-Leaved Alumroot (*H. cylindrica*) appears in the mountains. It has greenish-white to cream-coloured flowers.

Western Canada Violet
Viola canadensis

VIOLET FAMILY

This plant favours moist to fairly dry deciduous forests, floodplains and clearings. The flowers are held on aerial stems, and are white with yellow bases. The lower 3 petals have purple lines, and the upper 2 have a purplish tinge on back. The leaves are heart-shaped, long-stalked, decidedly pointed at the tip, and have saw-toothed edges. This small white flower splashes shady woods and marshes in the mid-summer.

The plant grows from short, thick rhizomes with slender creeping runners. These violets are easily propagated from runners or sections of rhizomes, and can be invasive in a garden setting. Violet flowers have long been used as a poultice for swellings. A similar species, Kidney-Leaved Violet (*V. renifolia*), occurs in similar habitat and also has a white flower with purplish veins. However, its leaves are kidney-shaped with blunt tips, and wavy and toothed margins.

Arrowhead (Wapato)
Sagittaria cuneata
WATER PLANTAIN FAMILY

Glen Lee Image

This perennial is an aquatic plant that grows up to 50 cm tall from tubers and slender rhizomes in shallow ponds, lakeshores, marshes, slow-moving water, and ditches, from the prairies to the montane zone. The submerged leaves are simple, narrow, and tapered at both ends. The emergent leaves are distinctive. They are large (up to 10 cm long and 6 cm wide), with long stalks, and are decidedly arrowhead-shaped. The plant produces both male and female flowers, and they are different. The female flowers (pistillate) tend to develop first, and are ball-like clusters on small stalks, appearing lower on the plant than do the male flowers. The male flowers (staminate) are showy, with 3 broadly oval white petals, and numerous stamens. The male flowers appear on long stalks.

The genus name, *Sagittaria*, is derived from the Latin *sagitta*, which means "arrow," a reference to the shape of the emergent leaves, and is the source of the common name. The species name, *cuneata*, means "wedge-shaped," and is said by most authorities to be a reference to the shape of the tuber. This is somewhat puzzling in that the tuber is more often described as resembling a walnut or golf ball. Wapato (sometimes spelled Wapatoo or Wappato) is the Chinook jargon trade language word for the tuber of this plant, it being, historically, a food source and trade item. Native peoples gathered the tubers with digging sticks, or with bare toes moved around in the mud where the plants grew. Members of the Lewis and Clark expedition ate the tubers while overwintering on the Columbia River in 1805, and allowed that they tasted of roasted potatoes. Other common names applied to the plant include Duck Potato, Indian Potato, and Swamp Potato.

Red, Orange, and Pink Flowers

This section contains flowers that are red, orange, or pink when encountered in the field. Flowers that are pinkish often can have tones running to lavender, so if you do not find the flower you are looking for, check the Blue/Purple section.

Common Hound's-Tongue
Cynoglossum officinale

BORAGE FAMILY

This coarse, hairy biennial weed was introduced from Europe and grows in disturbed ground and roadside ditches. It has a single leafy stem that grows to 80 cm in height. The leaves are alternate, elliptic to lance-shaped, tapered to slender stalks at the base of the plant, and becoming stalkless and clasping near the top of the plant. The flowers are reddish-purple and funnel-shaped, with 5 spreading lobes. The flowers appear from the upper leaf axils. The fruits are clusters of small nutlets that are covered with barbed prickles.

The genus name, *Cynoglossum*, is derived from the Greek *cynos*, meaning "dog," and *glossa*, meaning "tongue." The hooked spines on the fruits catch on clothing and fur, a mechanism for seed distribution. Some people experience skin irritation when they come into contact with the plant. In the words of the famous naturalist Lewis J. Clark: "The plant is coarse and unattractive."

Water Smartweed
Polygonum amphibium

BUCKWHEAT FAMILY

This plant occurs from prairie to subalpine elevations, and is found in ponds, marshes, ditches, and lakeshores, often forming mats in standing water. The plant may grow on land adjacent to or in the water. The leaves are large, oblong to lance-shaped, rounded or pointed at the tips, and have a prominent midvein. The flowers are pink and occur in a dense, oblong cluster at the top of thick, smooth stalks.

The species name, *amphibium*, refers to the aquatic habitat of the plant. The plant was used by Native peoples both medicinally—in poultices to treat piles and skin disease—and as a food source. The plant is also a food source for a large variety of birds.

Red Columbine
Aquilegia formosa
BUTTERCUP FAMILY

These beautiful flowers are found in meadows and dry to moist woods, and are among the showiest of all prairie wildflowers. The leaves of the plant are mostly basal and compound, with 3 sets of 3 leaflets each. The flowers occur on stems above the basal leaves, and the stem leaves are smaller than the basal leaves, only appearing with 3 leaflets each. The 5 petals have red spurs above, and yellow blades below. The 5 sepals are red. Numerous stamens extend well beyond the petal blades.

The origin of the common and genus names is discussed in the note on Blue Columbine (*A. brevistyla*), shown on page 73. The species name of the Red Columbine, *formosa*, means "comely" or "beautiful." Bumblebees and butterflies are drawn to the Columbines to collect the nectar. Columbines also appear in western North America in yellow (*A. flavescens*), but that species is generally restricted to higher elevations.

193

Cushion Cactus (Ball Cactus)
Coryphantha vivipara (also *Mamillaria vivipara*)

CACTUS FAMILY

This low-growing, squat perennial cactus grows singly or in clumps in dry, eroded, sandy, and rocky soils, often on south-facing slopes in the southern part of the area. Its pin-cushion stem rises only a few inches above the ground. The whole surface of the rounded stem is covered with evenly spaced, spine-tipped projections. The beautiful purplish to pink flowers have numerous lance-shaped petals, and occur between the spines. Each flower also has a shower of yellow stamens in the centre. The flowers are short-lived, and grow into round, soft, edible berries, which are consumed by antelope.

The genus name, *Coryphantha*, is derived from the Greek *koryphe*, which means "a cluster," and *anthos*, which means "flower," a reference to the blooming habit of the plant. The species name, *vivipara*, means "bearing live young," perhaps a reference to the ease of propagation of the species. The berries of the plant are said to taste like gooseberries, and can be made into a jam.

Bee Plant
Cleome serrulata

CAPER FAMILY

Cliff Wallis image

This erect, somewhat shrubby, malodorous plant grows up to 80 cm tall in disturbed places, on rodent mounds, and on roadsides, often appearing in large bunches. The lower leaves are compound and long-stalked, with 3 lance-shaped to oval leaflets that are smooth and dark green. The upper leaves are nearly stalkless, alternate, and lance-shaped. The flowers are pink to purplish, and occur in a rounded, elongated, terminal cluster at the top of the stem. The stamens are whitish and protruding. The inflorescence has the appearance of a bottle-brush.

The plant is attractive to bees, butterflies, and other insects because it produces large amounts of nectar. Many Native peoples used the plant as a food source, boiling the young shoots and leaves as a potherb. The residue left from the boiling was often used as a paint or dye on pottery. The plant was collected by the Lewis and Clark expedition near the Vermillion River in what is now South Dakota in 1804, and was described in their journal. It goes by several locally common names, including Spider Plant, Spider-Flower, Stinking Clover, Rocky Mountain Bee Plant, and Clammy Weed.

Dotted Blazingstar
Liatris punctata

COMPOSITE FAMILY

Anne Elliott image

This plant is a showy perennial that grows to 60 cm tall from a thickened rootstock, often forming clumps in dry grasslands, meadows, and hillsides in the southern prairies. The grey-green leaves are numerous, alternate, narrowly lance-shaped, entire, and have a prominent whitish midvein. The leaves are somewhat covered with translucent glandular dots or pits, giving rise to part of the common name. The flowers are rose-coloured to deep purple, and are arranged in a dense, crowded cluster of disk flowers, bunched at the top of the flowering stem. The individual flowers are tubular, five-lobed, and have protruding, curved stigmas.

The origin of the genus name, *Liatris*, is unknown. The species name, *punctata*, is a reference to the glands on the leaves, which have the appearance of dark puncture marks. This plant is also known in some locales as Dotted Gayfeather. A similar plant, Meadow Blazingstar (*L. ligulistylis*), occurs in the area, but prefers moister habitat, and has larger, rounder flower heads. Butterflies are frequent visitors to the Blazingstars. These plants should not be confused with Blazing Star (*Mentzelia laevicaulis*), discussed on page 119.

196

Flodman's Thistle
Cirsium flodmanii

COMPOSITE FAMILY

This perennial native thistle grows in coulees and at the bases of hills from a sturdy taproot, and can reach heights of up to a metre. The plant is covered in woolly hairs, giving it a white mottled appearance. The basal leaves are up to 15 cm long, while the stem leaves are shorter. The leaves are greenish above, grey woolly below, deeply incised, and covered with spines. The plant bears 1–5 large flower heads, purple in colour, and up to 5 cm broad.

The genus name, *Cirsium*, is derived from the Greek *kirsos*, which means "swollen vein," a reference to thistles once being thought to remedy that problem. The species name, *flodmanii*, is to honour J.H. Flodman, who discovered the plant. The plant is also known as Prairie Thistle. A similar plant, Wavy-Leaved Thistle (*C. undulatum*) occurs in the same habitat, but Flodman's Thistle is smaller and more delicate than Wavy-Leaved Thistle.

Spotted Knapweed
Centaurea maculosa

COMPOSITE FAMILY

This introduced noxious weed inhabits roadsides, ditches, and disturbed areas, and has become a problem in many locales. The plant is many-branched and grows up to over a metre tall from creeping rhizomes. The flowers are heads at the ends of branches, with dark pink or purple disk florets only.

The name Knapweed is derived from the ancient English *knap*, meaning "knob" or "bump," a reference to the bumps on the branches of the plant. The genus name, *Centaurea*, is derived from the Greek *kentaur*, the mythical beast believed to have healing powers. The species name, *maculosa*, means "spotted," a reference to the spots on the bracts of the flowers. It is believed that this plant was inadvertently introduced into North America when its seeds contaminated a shipment of forage crop seeds.

Black Gooseberry
Ribes lacustre

CURRANT FAMILY

An erect deciduous shrub, growing up to 1.5 m tall, which occurs in moist woods and open areas. The branches of the plant have small prickles and stout thorns at leaf and branch bases. The leaves are alternate and shaped like maple leaves, with 3–5 deeply cut palmate lobes. The flowers are reddish in colour, saucer-shaped, and hang in elongated clusters. The fruits are dark purple to black berries, which bristle with tiny hairs.

The genus *Ribes* contains all of the Gooseberries and Currants. Commonly, members of the *Ribes* genus are divided into Currants and Gooseberries depending upon whether or not the berries are bristly hairy—Currants are not bristly hairy, and Gooseberries are. The genus is large and complicated, and the particular species contained therein are difficult to identify without a botanical key. This species is included as an example, and is by no means the full extent of the genus found in the area. Key recognition features of the group are: clusters of red, blue, or black berries; maple-leaf shaped lobed leaves; and flowers and fruits that are hairy and/or bear sticky glands. The existence of locally common names further complicates the matter of identification. For example, Black Gooseberry is also known locally as Bristly Black Currant and Wild Black Currant. Other members of the genus also share those names in local parlance.

Fireweed
Epilobium angustifolium
EVENING PRIMROSE FAMILY

A plant of disturbed areas, roadsides, clearings, and shaded woods. This plant is often one of the first plants to appear after a fire. The pink, four-petaled flowers bloom in long terminal clusters. Bracts between the petals are narrow. The flowers bloom from the bottom of the cluster first, then upward on the stem. The leaves are alternate and appear whorled.

The genus name, *Epilobium*, is derived from the Greek *epi*, meaning "upon," and *lobos*, meaning "a pod," which refers to the position of the flowers on top of the seed pod. The species name, *angustifolium*, means "narrow-leafed." The common name originates from the plant's tendency to spring up from seeds and rhizomes on burned-over lands. The leaves resemble willow leaves, hence the alternate name Willowherb. The young leaves can be used in salads, and a weak tea can be brewed from the plant. The inner pith can be used to thicken soups and stews. Fireweed is the floral emblem of the Yukon Territory.

Scarlet Butterflyweed
Gaura coccinea

EVENING PRIMROSE FAMILY

This is a plant of grasslands and dry south-facing slopes. The flowers are whitish when they first bloom, becoming scarlet or pink as the flower ages. Usually only a few of the flowers on an individual plant bloom at once, and the flowers open fully only at night.

The genus name, *Gaura*, is derived from the Greek *gauros*, meaning "superb" or "proud," most probably a reference to the erect nature of the flowers. The species name, *coccinea*, means "scarlet," a reference to the colour of the flower. The common name arises most probably because the flowers are said to be shaped like butterflies.

Paintbrush
Castilleja miniata
FIGWORT FAMILY

A plant of alpine meadows, well-drained slopes, open subalpine forests, moist stream banks, and open foothills woods. Paintbrush is widely distributed and extremely variable in colour—from pink, to red, to yellow, to white. The leaves are narrow and sharp-pointed, linear to lance-shaped, usually without teeth or divisions, but sometimes the upper leaves have 3 shallow lobes. The showy red, leafy bracts, which are actually modified leaves, resemble a brush dipped in paint, hence the common name.

The genus name, *Castilleja*, commemorates Domingo Castillejo, an 18th-century Spanish botanist. The species name, *miniata*, refers to the scarlet-red colour minium, an oxide of lead. Although beautiful, this plant should not be transplanted as it is partially parasitic and does not survive transplanting well.

Strawberry Blite
Chenopodium capitatum

GOOSEFOOT FAMILY

This plant is found from low to subalpine elevations, and is distinctive for its large triangular or arrowhead-shaped leaves and its dense, fleshy clusters of bright red flowers. The flower clusters appear at the ends of branches on the plant, usually in interrupted bunches, and in the leaf axils.

The genus name, *Chenopodium*, is Greek for "goose foot," a reference to the leaf's resemblance to the foot of a goose. The leaves are rich in vitamins and minerals, and are said to resemble spinach when eaten. The flowers are also edible, though most authorities warn against over-indulging in consuming the plant. Some Native peoples used the red flowers as a source for dye, it being bright red initially, then darkening to purple as it ages. Another common name for the plant is Indian Paint.

Kinnikinnick (Bearberry)
Arctostaphylos uva-ursi
HEATH FAMILY

This trailing or matted evergreen shrub grows low to the ground, and has long branches with reddish, flaky bark and leathery, shiny green leaves. The flowers are pale pink and urn-shaped, appearing in clumps at the ends of the stems. The fruits are dull red berries.

The genus name, *Arctostaphylos*, is derived from the Greek *arktos*, meaning "bear," and *staphyle*, meaning "bunch of grapes." The species name, *uva-ursi*, is Latin for "bear's grape." The berries are apparently relished by bears and birds, though they tend to be dry and mealy to humans. They are edible and have been used as food, prepared in a variety of ways. The berries remain on the plant through the winter. One of the common names, Kinnikinnick, is believed to be of Algonquin origin, and means "something to smoke," a reference to the fact that some Native peoples used the leaves of the plant as a tobacco.

Pine-Drops
Pterospora andromedea

HEATH FAMILY

This purple or reddish-brown saprophyte (a plant that gets its nutrients from decaying plant or animal matter) stands up to a metre tall or more, and lives in deep humus of coniferous or mixed woods. The plants grow singly or in clusters, but they are rare. The leaves are mostly basal, and resemble scales. The stem stands erect, and is covered with glandular hairs. The flowers are cream-coloured to yellowish, and occur in a raceme that covers roughly the top half of the stalk. The petals are united into an urn shape, and hang downward off bent flower stalks, like small lanterns. The stalks of the plant will remain erect for a year or more after the plant dies.

The genus name, *Pterospora*, is derived from the Greek *pteron*, meaning "wing," and *sporos*, meaning "seed," a reference to the winged appearance of the seeds. The species name, *andromedea*, refers to Andromeda of Greek mythology. In Greek mythology, Cassiopeia was the wife of Cepheus, the King of the Ethiopians. She was vain and boastful, claiming that her beauty exceeded that of the sea nymphs. This claim offended and angered the sea nymphs, and they prevailed upon Poseidon, the God of the Sea, to send a sea monster to punish Cassiopeia by ravaging the land. In order to save the kingdom, the Ethiopians offered Cassiopeia's daughter, Andromeda, as a sacrifice, chaining her to a rock. Perseus, the Greek hero who slew the Gorgon Medusa, intervened at the last minute to free Andromeda and slay the monster. In astronomy, the constellation Perseus stands between Cassiopeia and Andromeda, still defending her today. While interesting, what brought the taxonomist to apply this name to this plant is a total mystery!

Pink Wintergreen
Pyrola asarifolia

HEATH FAMILY

An erect perennial that inhabits moist to dry coniferous and mixed forests, and riverine environments. The flowers are shaped like an inverted cup or bell, nodding, waxy, pale pink to purplish red, and have a long, curved, projecting style. The leaves are basal in a rosette. The leaves have a leathery appearance, and are shiny, rounded, and dark green.

The genus name, *Pyrola*, is derived from Latin *pyrus*, which means "a pear," probably a reference to the leaves being pear-shaped. The species name, *asarifolia*, is derived from the Latin *asarum*, meaning "ginger," and *folium*, meaning "leaf," a reference to the similarity between the leaves of this plant and those of wild ginger. Wintergreen leaves contain acids which are effective in treating skin irritations. Mashed leaves of *Pyrola* species have traditionally been used by herbalists in skin salves and poultices for snake and insect bites. They are called wintergreen, not because of the taste, but because the leaves remain green during the winter. Like orchids, many of these plants require a specific fungus in the soil to grow successfully, and transplantation should not be attempted. Two other species of *Pyrola*, Greenish-Flowered Wintergreen (*P. chlorantha*) and One-Sided Wintergreen (*P. secunda*) occur in similar habitat.

Nodding Onion
Allium cernuum

LILY FAMILY

All *Allium* species smell strongly of onion, and have small flower clusters at the top of the leafless stalk. Nodding Onion is a common species in the prairie region, and is easily identified by its pink drooping or nodding inflorescence. There are usually 8–12 flowers in the nodding cluster.

The stem gives off an oniony odour when crushed, and is said to be one of the better tasting wild onions. Native peoples gathered the bulbs and ate them raw and cooked; used them for flavouring other foods; and dried them for later use. Ground squirrels also use this plant in their diets. *Allium* is the Latin name for "garlic," from the Celtic *all*, meaning "hot" or "burning," because it irritates the eyes. The species name, *cernuum*, refers to the crook in the stem of the plant just below the flower. Another similar onion, the Pink-Flowered Onion (*A. stellatum*), appears in similar habitat. Pink-Flowered Onion holds the flowers erect, instead of nodding.

Western Wood Lily
Lilium philadelphicum (also *Lilium umbellatum*)

LILY FAMILY

This lily grows in moist meadows, dense to open woods, and edges of aspen groves, from prairie elevations to the low subalpine zone. The leaves are numerous, lance-shaped, smooth, and alternate on the stem, except for the upper leaves, which are in whorls. Each plant may produce from 1–5 bright orange to orange-red flowers, each with 3 petals and 3 similar sepals. The petals and the sepals are orange at the tip, becoming yellowish and black, or purple-dotted, at the bases. The anthers are dark purple in colour.

Lilium is the Latin name for the plant. There are several stories as to how the species name originates. One explanation holds that Linnaeus—the Swedish naturalist who invented binomial identification for plants—received his specimens of the plant from a student in Philadelphia. Another explanation holds that the name comes from the Greek words *philos*, meaning "love," and *delphicus*, the ancient wooded oracle at Delphi, hence "wood lover." The Western Wood Lily is the floral emblem of Saskatchewan, but it is becoming increasingly rare, owing to picking of the flower. The bulb from which the flower grows depends upon the flower for nutrients, and will die if the flower is picked. The plants do not survive transplantation well, but can be grown from seeds, though the propagated plants might not flower for several years. The bulbs were eaten by some Native tribes, but were generally considered to be bitter. The Blackfoot treated spider bites with a wet dressing of the crushed flowers. Western Wood Lily is often confused with Tiger Lily (*L. columbianum*), which are coloured similarly, but the petals on the Tiger Lily are curled backwards, while the petals on the Wood Lily are held in a chalice-shape.

Scarlet Mallow
Sphaeralcea coccinea

MALLOW FAMILY

This low-growing perennial grows up to 20 cm tall, and may appear singly or in large colonies. It grows from a branched, scaly, thick, woody rootstock, and occurs in grasslands, roadsides, railway rights-of-way, and other disturbed places. The leafy stems are prostrate, and spread out from the woody base to end in dense clusters of red flowers. The leaves are alternate and long-stalked, with several divisions and notches at the tips. The stems and leaves are covered with star-shaped clusters of fine, white hair, giving the whole plant a greyish-green appearance. The flowers are shaped like Hollyhocks, with 5 orange to brick red petals, which are notched at the tip, 5 sepals, and numerous stamens.

The genus name, *Sphaeralcea*, is derived from the Greek *sphaera*, meaning "a sphere," and *alcea*, a name of a plant in the Mallow Family. The reference to a sphere is probably to the rounded fruit of the plant. The species name, *coccinea*, is Latin for "scarlet." The common name, Mallow, is from a Greek word meaning "soft," most likely a reference to the feel of the leaves. Some Native peoples made a paste from the plant to treat scalds and burns.

Showy Milkweed
Asclepias speciosa

MILKWEED FAMILY

Anne Elliott image

This perennial plant is rather spectacular, with its tall coarse stem, large leaves, and round clusters of pink to purple flowers. It grows to heights of up to 2 m from a thick, creeping rootstock, often occurring in clumps. It is found in moist grasslands, along roadsides, in thickets, and along streams. The leaves are dark green, opposite, short-stalked, oblong or oval, thick, prominently veined, and rounded at the tip, sometimes having a sharp spine. The flowers have a strong scent, are purplish to pink, and occur in dense, rounded, umbrella-shaped clusters that can span 7 cm across. Each flower is up to 1 cm long, and the corolla is five-parted, with reflexed lobes that have the appearance of horns that curve inward.

The genus name, *Asclepias*, honours Asklepios, the Greek god of medicine, perhaps a reference to the plant's medicinal properties. The species name, *speciosa*, is Latin for "showy." The common name, Milkweed, arises because the plant exudes a milky latex when the stem is cut. This latex was allowed to harden, and then used as a chewing gum by some Native peoples. The plant contains alkaloids and resins in the stems and leaves, which may cause it to be poisonous to livestock. The plant is a host plant to Monarch Butterflies, the larvae of which feed on it, and are said to accumulate the alkaloids as a defence mechanism against predators.

Wild Bergamot
Monarda fistulosa
MINT FAMILY

This showy flower inhabits grasslands and open woods, blooming in the summer months. The stems of the plant are erect and square, with a strong and distinctive odour of mint. The stem is topped by a dense cluster of pink to violet flowers. The leaves are opposite, triangular to ovate in shape, and pointed at the ends.

Native peoples used Bergamot medicinally for various ailments, from acne, to bronchial complaints, to stomach pains. Some tribes used the plant as a perfume, meat preservative, and insect repellant. It is also reported that the plant was used ceremonially in the Sun Dance. The genus name, *Monarda*, honours an early Spanish physician, Nicholas Monardez, who described many North American plants. The species name, *fistulosa*, means "tubular," a reference to the flower shape. Local common names include Horsemint, Bee Balm, and Oswego Tea.

Red Clover
Trifolium pratense
PEA FAMILY

A European species now well established in North America, Red Clover grows to heights of 60 cm in low to mid-elevations. The leaves are in threes, often displaying a white crescent-shaped spot near the base. The flowers are pea-like, pinkish to purple, and up to 200 of them occur in a dense head, 2–3 cm in diameter, at stem tops. Two leaves lie immediately below the flower head.

All clovers have leaves in threes and flowers in dense heads. The name Clover is derived from the Latin *clava*, meaning "club," and more particularly the triple-headed cudgel carried by Hercules. That club bears a resemblance to the shape of the leaf on Clover. The suit of clubs in cards is from the same root, and has the same shape. White Clover (*T. repens*) is a similar plant in the same habitat. White Clover has a creeping stem and white to pinkish flowers on longer stalks. Herbalists favour Red Clover in the treatment of skin problems.

Pitcher Plant
Sarracenia purpurea
PITCHER PLANT FAMILY

Glen Lee image

This unique and unusual plant has wide distribution in eastern North America, but is fairly rare in the prairie provinces. It grows in sedge fens and bogs. The evergreen leaves are arranged in a basal rosette that has been modified to form a pitcher that stands up to 30 cm tall. The "spout" of the pitcher stands upright, and the leaves forming the vessel have strong red venations. The pitcher holds water. The flowers are wine-red to dark red, have 5 sepals, and appear solitary and nodding on a leafless stem that rises from the rhizome.

The genus name, *Sarracenia*, honours Michael Sarrasin, an early French botanist and physician. The species name, *purpurea*, is Latin for "purple," and is probably a reference to the flower or leaf colour. This plant is carnivorous. Red veins lead down from the top of the pitcher to nectar inside. When insects follow the veins, they encounter downward pointing hairs in the curved throat of the pitcher, where they slip into the water in the pitcher. The plant then digests them. Spiders, and even small frogs, are also eaten by the plant. This plant is the floral emblem of the Province of Newfoundland. Its common names are numerous, and include Purple Pitcher Plant, Flytrap, Sidesaddle Plant, Huntsman's Cup, Indian Cup, Indian Jug, Indian Pipe, and Frog's Britches.

Sea Milkwort
Glaux maritima
PRIMROSE FAMILY

Glen Lee image

This low-growing relatively uncommon perennial is erect and leafy-stemmed, and grows to only 15 cm tall at the edges of saline marshes, slough margins, on lakeshores, and in moist meadows. The branching stems arise from a creeping rootstock, and each stem has numerous leaves. The leaves are opposite, oval to narrowly oblong, light green in colour, succulent, and stalkless. The flowers occur in the leaf axils, and are white to pinkish, cup-shaped with 5 lobes, and composed only of tiny petal-like sepals, which enclose the stamens.

The genus name, *Glaux*, is derived from the Greek *glaukos*, which means "bluish-green," a reference to the colour of the leaves. The species name, *maritima*, means "of the sea," and is probably a reference to plant's existence in coastal habitat. Some Native peoples were said to eat the roots of this plant to induce sleepiness, but overdoing that causes sickness. The common name might present some confusion. This plant is not related to the Milkwort Family.

Prickly Rose
Rosa acicularis

ROSE FAMILY

The floral emblem of the Province of Alberta, the Prickly Rose is a deciduous shrub with freely branched stems and thorns at the base of each leaf. The flowers are pink with 5 broad petals. Leaves are oblong and notched, somewhat hairy below. The Prickly Rose will easily hybridize with other members of the Rose Family, and can be difficult to specifically identify. The fruits are dark red, round to oval, fleshy hips, with sepals remaining on top, like a beard. They are high in vitamin C content, and can be a favourite food of many species of birds. The hips can be used to make a delicious jelly.

The foliage and young stems of wild roses are browsed by wild ungulates and domestic livestock. Native peoples used the plants for medicinal purposes, and used the thorns for fishing lures. Wild Roses produce root suckers, and can be very invasive and aggressive in spreading.

Three-Flowered Avens (Old Man's Whiskers, Prairie Smoke)
Geum triflorum

ROSE FAMILY

This plant is widespread on dry plateaus at low to subalpine elevations, open grasslands, and arid basins. The flowers bloom in early spring, and are dull purplish to pinkish, hairy, and nodding at the top of the stem. The flowers usually occur in a cluster of 3, though some plants will have as many as 5 flowers on a single stem. The flowers remain semi-closed and do not open out flat. They were once described to me as "looking like 3 very tired ballerinas at the close of a performance."

Old Man's Whiskers is probably a reference to the appearance of the fruits—achenes with feathery styles—that resemble grey whiskers. These fruits are distributed by winds, and it is said that they sometimes occurred in such abundance on the unbroken prairies that when the seeds blew, it looked like smoke over the prairies, hence another common name, Prairie Smoke. Some Native peoples boiled the roots to make a tea to use as a medicine for colds, flu, and fever.

GLOSSARY

Achene: A dry, single-seeded fruit that does not split open at maturity

Alkaloid: Any of a group of complex, nitrogen-based chemicals, often found in plants, that are thought to protect the plants against insect predation. Many of these substances are poisonous

Alternate: A reference to the arrangement of leaves on a stem where the leaves appear singly and staggered on opposite sides of the stem

Annual: A plant that completes its life cycle, from seed germination to production of new seed, within a year and then dies

Anther: The portion of the stamen (the male portion of a flower) that produces pollen

Axil: The upper angle formed where a leaf, branch, or other organ is attached to a plant stem

Basal: A reference to leaves that are found at the base or bottom of the plant, usually near ground level

Berry: A fleshy, many-seeded fruit

Biennial: A plant that completes its life cycle in two years, normally producing leaves in the first year, but not producing flowers until the second year, then dies

Blade: The body of a leaf, excluding the stalk

Bract: A reduced or otherwise modified leaf that is usually found near the flower or inflorescence of a plant, but is not part of the flower or inflorescence

Bristle: A stiff hair, usually erect or curving away from its attachment point

Bulb: An underground plant part derived from a short, often rounded shoot that is covered with scales or leaves

Calcareous: In reference to soils, containing calcium carbonate

Calyx: The outer set of flower parts, usually composed of sepals

Capsule: A dry fruit with more than one compartment that splits open to release seeds

Clasping: In reference to a leaf, surrounding or partially wrapping around a stem or branch

Cluster: A grouping or close arrangement of individual flowers that is not dense and continuous

Composite inflorescence: A flower-like inflorescence of the Composite Family, composed of ray and/or disk flowers. Where both ray and disk flowers are present, the ray flowers surround the disk flowers

Compound leaf: A leaf that is divided into two or many leaflets, each of which may look like a complete leaf, but which lacks buds. Compound leaves may have a variety of arrangements. Pinnate leaves have leaflets arranged like a feather, with attachment to a central stem. Palmate leaves have leaflets radiating from a common point, like the fingers of a hand

Corm: An enlarged base or stem resembling a bulb

Corolla: The collective term for the petals of the flower that are found inside the sepals

Cultivar: A cultivated variety of a wild plant

Cyme: A broad, flat-topped flower arrangement in which the inner, central flowers bloom first

Decumbent: In reference to a plant, reclining or lying on the ground, with tip ascending

Decurrent: In reference to a leaf, extending down from the point of insertion on the stem, so when the edges of the leaf continue down the stem, they form wings on the stem

Disk flower: Any of the small tubular florets found in the central clustered portion of the flower head of members of the Composite Family; also referred to as "disk florets"

Dioecious: Having unisex flowers, where male and female flowers appear on separate plants; see *monoecious*

Drupe: A fleshy or juicy fruit that covers a single, stony seed inside, e.g., a cherry or peach

Drupelet: Any one part of an aggregate fruit (like a raspberry or blackberry), where each such part is a fleshy fruit that covers a single, stony seed inside

Elliptic: Ellipse-shaped, widest in the middle

Elongate: Having a slender form, long in relation to width

Entire: In reference to a leaf, a leaf edge that is smooth, without teeth or notches

Filament: The part of the stamen that supports the anther. Also can refer to any threadlike structure

Florescence: Generally the flowering part of a plant; the arrangement of the flowers on the stem; also referred to as "inflorescence"

Floret: One of the small tubular flowers in the central, clustered portion of the flower head of members of the Composite Family; also known as "disk flower"

Flower head: A dense and continuous group of flowers without obvious branches or spaces between

Follicle: A dry fruit composed of a single compartment that splits open along one side at maturity to release seeds

Fruit: The ripe ovary with the enclosed seeds, and any other structures that enclose it

Gland: A small organ that secretes a sticky or oily substance, and is attached to some part of the plant

Glandular hairs: Small hairs attached to glands on plants

Glaucous: With a fine, waxy, often white coating that may be rubbed off; often characteristic of leaves, fruits, and stems

Hood: in reference to flower structure, a curving or folded, petal-like structure interior to the petals and exterior to the stamens in certain flowers

Host: In reference to a parasitic or semi-parasitic plant, the plant from which the parasite obtains its nourishment

Inflorescence: Generally the flowering part of a plant; the arrangement of the flowers on the stem; also referred to as "florescence"

Involucral bract: A modified leaf found just below an inflorescence

Keel: A ridge or fold, shaped like the bottom of a boat, which may refer to leaf structure, or more often to the two fused petals in flowers that are members of the Pea Family

Lance-shaped: In reference to leaf shape, much longer than wide, widest below the middle and tapering to the tip, like the blade of a lance

Leaflet: A distinct, leaflike segment of a compound leaf

Linear: Like a line; long, narrow, and parallel-sided

Lobe: A reference to the arrangement of leaves, a segment of a divided plant part, typically rounded

Margin: The edge of a leaf or petal

Mat: A densely interwoven or tangled, low, ground-hugging growth

Midrib: The main rib of a leaf

Midvein: The middle vein of a leaf

Monoecious: A plant having unisex flowers, with separate male and female flowers on the same plant; see *dioecious*

Nectary: A plant structure that produces and secretes nectar

Node: A joint on a stem or root

Noxious weed: A plant, usually imported, that out-competes and drives out native plants

Oblong: Somewhat rectangular, with rounded ends

Obovate: Shaped like a teardrop

Opposite: A reference to the arrangement of leaves on a stem where the leaves appear paired on opposite sides of the stem, directly across from each other

Oval: Broadly elliptic

Ovary: The portion of the flower where the seeds develop. It is usually a swollen area below the style and stigma

Ovate: Egg shaped

Palmate: A reference to the arrangement of leaves on a stem where the leaves spread like the fingers on a hand, diverging from a central or common point

Panicle: A branched inflorescence that blooms from the bottom up

Pappus: The cluster of bristles, scales, or hairs at the top of an achene in the flowers of the Composite Family

Pencilled: Marked with coloured lines, like the petals on Violets

Perennial: A plant that does not produce seeds or flowers until its second year of life, then lives for three or more years, usually flowering each year before dying

Petal: A component of the inner floral portion of a flower, often the most brightly coloured and visible part of the flower

Petiole: The stem of a leaf

Pinnate: A reference to the arrangement of leaves on a stem where the leaves appear in two rows on opposite sides of a central stem, similar to the construction of a feather

Pistil: The female member of a flower that produces seed, consisting of the ovary, the style, and the stigma. A flower may have one to several separate pistils

Pistillate: A flower with female reproductive parts, but no male reproductive parts

Pod: A dry fruit

Pollen: The tiny, often powdery, male reproductive microspores formed in the stamens and necessary for sexual reproduction in flowering plants

Pome: A fruit with a core, e.g., an apple or pear

Prickle: A small, sharp, spiny outgrowth from the outer surface

Raceme: A flower arrangement that has an elongated flower cluster with the flowers attached to short stalks of relatively equal length that are attached to the main central stalk

Ray flower: One of the outer strap-shaped petals seen in members of the Composite Family. Ray flowers may surround disk flowers or may comprise the whole of the flower head; also referred to as "ray florets"

Reflexed: Bent backwards, often in reference to petals, bracts, or stalks

Rhizome: An underground stem that produces roots and shoots at the nodes

Riverine: Moist habitats along rivers or streams

Rootstock: Short, erect, underground stem, from which new leaves and shoots are produced annually

Rosette: A dense cluster of basal leaves from a common underground part, often in a flattened, circular arrangement

Runner: A long, trailing or creeping stem

Saprophyte: An organism that obtains its nutrients from dead organic matter

Sepal: A leaf-like appendage that surrounds the petals of a flower. Collectively the sepals make up the calyx

Serrate: Possessing sharp, forward-pointing teeth

Sessile: Of leaves, attached directly to the base, without a stalk

Shrub: A multi-stemmed woody plant

Simple leaf: A leaf that has a single leaf-like blade, which may be lobed or divided

Spike: An elongated, unbranched cluster of stalkless or nearly stalkless flowers

Spine: A thin, stiff, sharp-pointed projection

Spur: A hollow, tubular projection arising from the base of a petal or sepal, often producing nectar

Spurred corolla: A corolla that has spurs

Stalk: The stem supporting the leaf, flower, or flower cluster

Stamen: The male member of the flower that produces pollen, typically consisting of an anther and a filament

Staminate: A flower with male reproductive parts, but no female reproductive parts

Staminode: A sterile stamen

Standard: The uppermost petal of a typical flower in the Pea Family

Stigma: The portion of the pistil receptive to pollination; usually at the top of the style, and often sticky or fuzzy

Stipule: An appendage, usually in pairs, found at the base of a leaf or leaf stalk

Stolon: A creeping, above-ground stem capable of sending up a new plant

Style: A slender stalk connecting the stigma to the ovary in the female organ of a flower

Talus: Loose, fragmented rock rubble usually found at the base of a rock wall, also known as "scree"

Taproot: A stout main root that extends downward

Tendril: A slender, coiled, or twisted filament with which climbing plants attach to their supports

Tepals: Petals and sepals that cannot be distinguished from one another

Terminal flower head: A flower that appears at the top of a stem, as opposed to originating from a leaf axil

Ternate: Arranged in threes, often in reference to leaf structures

Toothed: Bearing teeth or sharply angled projections along the edge

Trailing: Lying flat on the ground, but not rooting

Tuber: A thick, creeping, underground stem

Tubular: Hollow or cylindrical, usually in reference to a fused corolla

Umbel: A flower arrangement where the flower stalks have a common point of attachment to the stem, like the spokes of an umbrella

Unisexual: Some flowers are unisexual, having either male parts or female parts, but not both. Some plants are unisexual, having either male flowers or female flowers, but not both

Urn-shaped: Hollow and cylindrical or globular, contracted at the mouth; like an urn

Vacuole: A membrane-bound compartment in a plant that is typically filled with liquid, and may perform various functions in the plant

Vein: A small tube that carries water, nutrients, and minerals, usually in reference to leaves

Whorl: Three or more parts attached at the same point along a stem or axis, often surrounding the stem; forming a ring radiating out from a common point

Wings: Side petals that flank the keel in typical flowers of the Pea Family

PLANT FAMILIES ARRANGED ACCORDING TO COLOUR

BLUE & PURPLE FLOWERS

Bladderwort Family
   Common Butterwort
Bluebell Family
   Kalm's Lobelia
Borage Family
   Blueweed
   Stickseed
   Tall Lungwort (Mertensia)
Buttercup Family
   Blue Clematis
   Blue Columbine
   Low Larkspur
   Prairie Crocus
Composite Family
   Blue Lettuce
   Bull Thistle
   Canada Thistle
   Common Burdock
   Parry's Townsendia
   Showy Aster
   Smooth Blue Aster
   Smooth Fleabane
Figwort Family
   Lilac-Flowered Beardtongue
   Small-Flowered Beardtongue
   Smooth Blue Beardtongue
Flax Family
   Blue Flax
Four-O'Clock Family
   Hairy Four-O'Clock
      (Umbrellawort)
Gentian Family
   Northern Gentian
   Oblong-Leaved Gentian
      (Prairie Gentian)
Geranium Family
   Sticky Purple Geranium
Harebell Family
   Harebell
Heath Family
   Western Bog-Laurel
      (Swamp Laurel)

Iris Family
   Blue-Eyed Grass
Mint Family
   Giant Hyssop
   Heal-All (Self-Heal)
   Marsh Hedge-Nettle
   Marsh Skullcap
   Wild Mint (Canada Mint)
Mustard Family
   Dame's Rocket (Dame's Violet)
Orchid Family
   Spotted Coralroot
   Striped Coralroot
   Venus Slipper
Pea Family
   Ascending Purple Milk-Vetch
   Indian Breadroot
   Purple Milk-Vetch
   Purple Prairie-Clover
   Showy Locoweed
   Silky Lupine
   Two-Grooved Milk-Vetch
Primrose Family
   Shooting Star
Rose Family
   Purple Avens
Violet Family
   Bog Violet
   Crowfoot Violet (Prairie Violet)
   Early Blue Violet
Waterleaf Family
   Thread-Leaved Phacelia
      (Thread-Leaved
      Scorpionweed)

RED, ORANGE & PINK FLOWERS

Borage Family
   Common Hound's-Tongue
Buckwheat Family
   Water Smartweed
Buttercup Family
   Red Columbine

Cactus Family
    Cushion Cactus (Ball Cactus)
Caper Family
    Bee Plant
Composite Family
    Dotted Blazingstar
    Flodman's Thistle
    Spotted Knapweed
Currant Family
    Black Gooseberry
Evening Primrose Family
    Fireweed
    Scarlet Butterflyweed
Figwort Family
    Paintbrush
Goosefoot Family
    Strawberry Blite
Heath Family
    Kinnikinnick (Bearberry)
    Pine-Drops
    Pink Wintergreen
Lily Family
    Nodding Onion
    Western Wood Lily
Mallow Family
    Scarlet Mallow
Milkweed Family
    Showy Milkweed
Mint Family
    Wild Bergamot
Pea Family
    Red Clover
Pitcher Plant Family
    Pitcher Plant
Primrose Family
    Sea Milkwort
Rose Family
    Prickly Rose
    Three-Flowered Avens
      (Old Man's Whiskers,
      Prairie Smoke)

WHITE, GREEN & BROWN FLOWERS
Arum Family
    Water Calla (Water Arum)
Blazing Star Family
    Evening Star
Borage Family
    Clustered Oreocarya
Buck-Bean Family
    Buck-Bean (Bog-Bean)
Buckwheat Family
    Narrow-Leaved Dock
Buttercup Family
    Water Crowfoot
      (Water Buttercup)
    Baneberry
    Canada Anemone
    Western Clematis
    Wind Flower
Carrot Family
    Cow Parsnip
    Water Hemlock
Cattail Family
    Common Cattail
Composite Family
    Arrow-Leaved Sweet Coltsfoot
    Ox-Eye Daisy
    Pineapple Weed
    Tufted Fleabane
    Yarrow
Currant Family
    Northern Gooseberry
Dogbane Family
    Spreading Dogbane
Dogwood Family
    Bunchberry (Dwarf Dogwood)
    Red Osier Dogwood
Evening Primrose Family
    Gumbo Evening-Primrose
      (Butte-Primrose)
Ginseng Family
    Wild Sarsaparilla
Grass-of-Parnassus Family
    Grass-of-Parnassus

Heath Family
    Blueberry (Canada Blueberry)
    Bog Cranberry
    Greenish-Flowered Wintergreen
    Indian-Pipe (Ghost Plant)
    Labrador Tea
    One-Sided Wintergreen
    Single Delight
Honeysuckle Family
    Low-Bush Cranberry
      (Mooseberry)
    Snowberry
    Twinflower
Lily Family
    Carrion Flower
    Death Camas
    Fairybells
    False Solomon's-Seal
    Prairie Onion
    White Camas
Madder Family
    Northern Bedstraw
    Sweet-Scented Bedstraw
Milkwort Family
    Seneca Snakeroot
Morning Glory Family
    Morning Glory
Mustard Family
    Pennycress (Stinkweed)
Nightshade Family
    Black Henbane
Orchid Family
    Hooded Ladies' Tresses
    Round-Leaved Orchid
    Sparrow's-Egg Lady's Slipper
      (Franklin's Lady's Slipper)
Pea Family
    Ground-Plum
    White Clover (Dutch Clover)
    White Peavine
    Wild Licorice
Phlox Family
    Moss Phlox

Pink Family
    Field Chickweed
      (Mouse-Ear Chickweed)
    Night-Flowering Catchfly
Primrose Family
    Mealy Primrose
Purslane Family
    Western Spring Beauty
Rose Family
    Birch-Leaf Spirea
    Black Hawthorn
    Chokecherry
    Pin Cherry
    Saskatoon (Serviceberry)
    Trailing Raspberry
    White Cinquefoil
    Wild Red Raspberry
    Wild Strawberry
Sandalwood Family
    Pale Comandra
      (Bastard Toadflax)
Saxifrage Family
    Richardson's Alumroot
Violet Family
    Western Canada Violet
Water Plantain Family
    Arrowhead (Wapato)

YELLOW FLOWERS

Bladderwort Family
    Common Bladderwort
Borage Family
    Puccoon (Lemonweed)
    Western False Gromwell
Broom-Rape Family
    Clustered Broom-Rape
Buckwheat Family
    Yellow Buckwheat
      (Umbrella Plant)
Buttercup Family
    Creeping Buttercup
      (Seaside Buttercup)
    Marsh-Marigold
    Meadow Buttercup

Cactus Family
    Prickly-Pear Cactus
Carrot Family
    Heart-Leaved Alexanders
      (Meadow Parsnip)
    Leafy Musineon
    Snakeroot
Composite Family
    Annual Hawk's-Beard
    Arrow-Leaved Balsamroot
    Black-Eyed Susan
    Broomweed (Snakeweed)
    Brown-Eyed Susan
    Colorado Rubber Weed
    Common Tansy
    Dandelion
    Goat's-Beard
    Gumweed
    Hairy Golden Aster
    Heart-Leaved Arnica
    Late Goldenrod
    Marsh Ragwort
    Narrow-Leaved Hawkweed
    Nodding Beggarticks
    Perennial Sow-Thistle
    Prairie Coneflower
    Prairie Groundsel
      (Woolly Groundsel)
    Prairie Sunflower
    Shining Arnica (Orange Arnica)
    Short-Beaked Agoseris
      (False Dandelion)
    Sneezeweed
    Stemless Rubber Weed
      (Butte Marigold)
Evening Primrose Family
    Yellow Evening-Primrose
Figwort Family
    Butter and Eggs
    Common Mullein
    Yellow Beardtongue
    Yellow Monkeyflower

Fumitory Family
    Golden Corydalis
Honeysuckle Family
    Twining Honeysuckle
Lily Family
    Yellowbell
Mustard Family
    Prairie Rocket
    Sand Bladderpod
Oleaster Family
    Soopolallie
      (Canadian Buffaloberry)
    Wolf Willow (Silverberry)
Orchid Family
    Yellow Lady's Slipper
Pea Family
    Buffalo Bean (Golden Bean)
    Caragana
    Cushion Milk-Vetch
    Field Locoweed
    Yellow Hedysarum
    Yellow Sweet-Clover
Primrose Family
    Fringed Loosestrife
Rose Family
    Agrimony
    Early Cinquefoil
    Shrubby Cinquefoil
    Silverweed
Stonecrop Family
    Narrow-Petaled Stonecrop
Touch-Me-Not Family
    Jewelweed (Touch-Me-Not)
Violet Family
    Yellow Prairie Violet
Water Lily Family
    Yellow Pond Lily
      (Yellow Water Lily)

Photograph credits

All photographs are by the author except those listed below, with sincere thanks by the author to the photographers for their gracious permission to use their work in this book.

Anne Elliott
Butter and Eggs page 39
Common Tansy page 20
Dotted Blazingstar page 196
Fringed Loosestrife page 57
Grass-of-Parnassus page 142
Gumweed page 23
Indian Breadroot page 105
Purple Avens page 112
Purple Prairie-Clover page 107
Showy Milkweed page 210
Silverweed page 61
Smooth Fleabane page 83
*Two-Grooved Milk-Vetch
     page 110*
Margot Hervieux
Bog Cranberry page 144
Buck-Bean page 121
Colin Ladyka
Black-Eyed Susan page 16
Crowfoot Violet page 114
Marsh Ragwort page 27
Yellow Prairie Violet page 64

Glen Lee
Arrowhead page 189
Blueberry page 143
Carrion Flower page 153
Colorado Rubberweed page 19
Common Butterwort page 67
Evening Star page 119
*Gumbo Evening-Primrose
     page 140*
Jewelweed page 63
Kalm's Lobelia page 68
*Lilac-Flowered Beardtongue
     page 84*
Nodding Beggarticks page 29
Oblong-Leaved Gentian page 90
Pitcher Plant page 213
Sea Milkwort page 214
Sneezeweed page 36
Elaine Nepstad
Water Calla page 118
Cliff Wallis
Bee Plant page 195

BIBLIOGRAPHY

Clark, L.J. and J. Trelawny (eds.), 1973, 1976, 1998. *Wildflowers of the Pacific Northwest.* Harbour Publishing, Madeira Park, British Columbia.

Cormack, R.G.H., 1977. *Wild Flowers of Alberta.* Hurtig Publishers, Edmonton, Alberta.

Kershaw, L., A. MacKinnon and J. Polar, 1998. *Plants of the Rocky Mountains.* Lone Pine Publishing, Edmonton, Alberta.

Parish, R., R. Coupe and D. Lloyd (eds.), 1996. *Plants of Southern Interior British Columbia.* Lone Pine Publishing, Edmonton, Alberta. ll

Phillips, W. H., 2001. *Northern Rocky Mountain Wildflowers.* Falcon, Helena, Montana.

Scotter, G. W., H. Flygare, 1986. *Wildflowers of the Canadian Rockies.* Hurtig Publishers Ltd., Toronto, Ontario.

Vance, F. R., J. R. Jowsey and J. S. McLean, 1977. *Wildflowers Across the Prairies.* Western Producer Prairie Books, Saskatoon, Saskatchewan.

Wilkinson, K., 1999. *Wildflowers of Alberta.* The University of Alberta Press and Lone Pine Publishing, Edmonton, Alberta.

Appendix

There are two plant families that are well-represented in this book that probably deserve some special attention—the Composite Family and the Pea Family.

The Composite Family (also known as Sunflower Family) is a very large plant family. In fact, it is one of the largest plant families, with over 20,000 species worldwide. Some are annuals, some are biennials, and some are perennials. Members of this family have flower heads that occur on the broadened top of the stem. Each flower head is composed of ray flowers (ray florets) and/or disk flowers (disk florets), attached to a common base, which is called a receptacle. Some species have both ray and disk flowers; some have ray flowers only; and some have disk flowers only. Ray flowers are generally strap-like, and disk flowers are tubular and five-lobed at the tip. Attached to the rim and surrounding the flower head is a series of scale or leaf-like bracts, which is called the involucre. These bracts may be sticky glandular, or they may have spines. The fruits of Composites are single seeds called achenes, which often have a pappus—a cluster of hairs, bristles, or scales—at the top. The pappus may assist in seed dispersal, by wind or by attachment to passing humans and animals.

Some groups in the Composite Family can be difficult to identify. Perhaps the best example of that difficulty is seen in the Fleabanes and the Asters. Fleabanes are often referred to as Daisies. Fleabanes usually flower earlier than do Asters, but blooming times can overlap. Fleabanes are usually shorter and have fewer leaves and flowers than Asters. Fleabanes tend to have more and narrower ray flowers than Asters. The best way to determine whether you are dealing with a Fleabane or an Aster, however, is to closely examine the involucral bracts of the specimen—even resorting to some magnification. The bracts in Fleabanes are arranged in a single row and are usually equal in length. The bracts in Asters occur in several rows, are stiffer and thicker, often display a white base and green tips, and overlap like shingles.

The Pea Family (also known as Legumes) is also a very large plant family, with about 14,000 species worldwide. Many of these are cultivated species, and have been food sources for thousands of years. Members of the Pea Family are most easily recognized by their flowers, which have a very distinctive shape. The flowers are composed of 5 highly differentiated petals. The uppermost petal is called a standard (or banner). It is usually the largest and showiest petal. Below the standard are 2 side petals called wings. The 2 lowest petals are fused together, forming the keel. The keel typically encloses the 10 stamens, 9 of which are generally fused into a tube. The fruits of members of the Pea Family are enclosed in a characteristic seed pod, known as a legume. Legumes split in two when mature, releasing the seeds into the environment. Most members of the Pea Family have compound leaves. Some are palmately compound, like the fingers on a hand. Lupines are a good example of such leaf construction. Other pea species have pinnately divided leaves, with leaflets arranged in opposite pairs along the stem. Some species have a modified leaf called a tendril, which allows the plant to attach itself to supports and thereby climb. Members of the Pea Family can contribute greatly to soil nutrients. They have nodules on their roots that contain nitrogen-fixing bacteria that convert atmospheric nitrogen into compounds the plant can utilize. In this way the soil is enriched.

INDEX

Photo by Dennis Hall

Neil Jennings is an ardent fly fisher, hiker, and photographer who loves "getting down in the dirt" to gaze at wildflowers. For twenty-two years he co-owned Country Pleasures, a fly fishing retailer in Calgary. He fly fishes extensively, both in fresh and salt water, and his angling pursuits usually lead him to wildflower investigations in a variety of venues. He has taught fly fishing courses in Calgary for over twenty years, and his photographs and writings on the subject have appeared in a number of outdoor magazines. Neil lives in Calgary with Linda, his wife of more than thirty years. They spend countless hours outdoors together, chasing fish, flowers, and – as often as possible – grandchildren.